OCS Study
MMS 2003-041

Coastal Marine Institute

# Changing Patterns of Ownership and Control in the Petroleum Industry: Implications for the Market for Oil and Gas Leases in the Gulf of Mexico OCS Region, 1983-1999

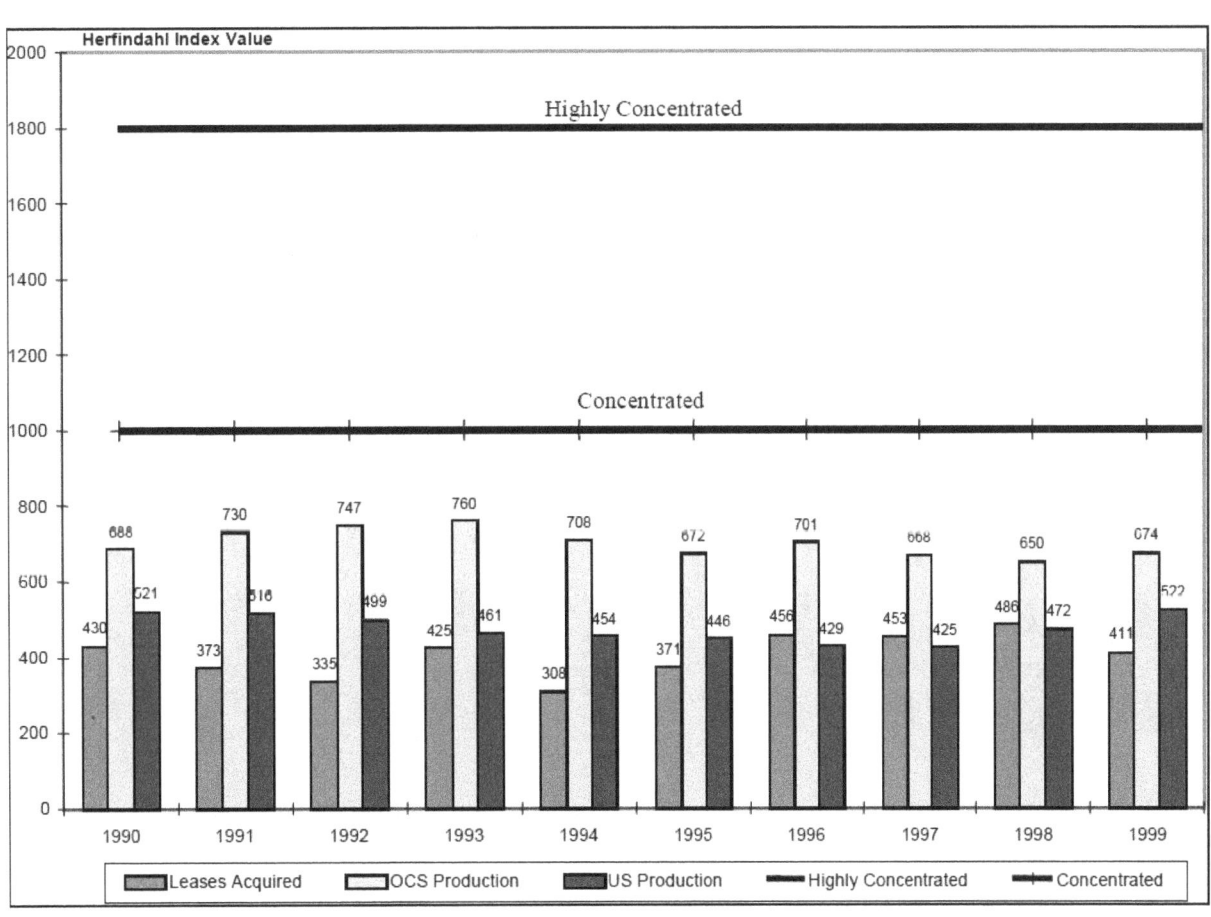

U.S. Department of the Interior
Minerals Management Service
Gulf of Mexico OCS Region

Cooperative Agreement
Coastal Marine Institute
Louisiana State University

OCS Study
MMS 2003-041

Coastal Marine Institute

# Changing Patterns of Ownership and Control in the Petroleum Industry: Implications for the Market for Oil and Gas Leases in the Gulf of Mexico OCS Region, 1983-1999

Authors

Allan G. Pulsipher
Omowumi O. Iledare
Dmitry V. Mesyanzhinov

October 2003

Prepared under MMS Contract
14-35-0001-30951-16806
by
The Center for Energy Studies
Louisiana State University
Baton Rouge, Louisiana 70803

Published by

**U.S. Department of the Interior**
**Minerals Management Service**
**Gulf of Mexico OCS Region**

Cooperative Agreement
Coastal Marine Institute
Louisiana State University

## DISCLAIMER

This report was prepared under contract between the Minerals Management Service (MMS) and Louisiana State University's Center for Energy Studies. This draft report has not been technically reviewed by MMS. Approval does not signify that the contents necessarily reflect the view and policies of the Service, nor does mention of trade names or commercial products constitute endorsement or recommendation for use. It is, however, exempt from review and compliance with MMS editorial standards.

## REPORT AVAILABILITY

Extra copies of the report may be obtained from the Public Information Office (Mail Stop 5034) at the following address:

U.S. Department of the Interior
Minerals Management Services
Gulf of Mexico OCS Region
Public Information Office (MS 5034)
1201 Elmwood Park Boulevard
New Orleans, Louisiana 70123-2394
Telephone Number: 1-800-200-GULF

## CITATION

Suggested Citation:

Pulsipher, A.G., O.O. Iledare, and D.V. Mesyanzhinov. 2003. Changing Patterns of Ownership and Control in the Petroleum Industry: Implications for the Market for Oil and Gas Leases in the Gulf of Mexico OCS Region, 1983-1999. Prepared by the Center for Energy Studies, Louisiana State University, Baton Rouge, LA. U.S. Dept. of the Interior, Minerals Management Service, Gulf of Mexico OCS Region, New Orleans, LA. OCS Study MMS 2003-041. 86 pp.

## ACKNOWLEDGMENTS

This report is based primarily on OCS leasing records made available to the Center for Energy Studies by the Minerals Management Service, New Orleans. Barbara Kavanaugh, Versa Stickle, Ric Pincomb, Yan Zhang, and Williams Olatubi were very helpful in obtaining and processing these data.

# ABSTRACT

Has consolidation of ownership and control in the petroleum industry reduced the extent of competition for or lowered the value of oil and gas leases on the Gulf of Mexico OCS?

Neither aggregate measures used by economists to analyze concentrated market and industry structures, nor patterns of joint bidding and cooperation among firms active in the offshore Gulf of Mexico suggest either a decrease or a deficiency in the competitiveness of the lease sales held by the U.S. Minerals Management Service (MMS). Whether leases acquired at the sales, or production by firms bidding for leases, are used as the base of the concentration measures, they indicate a competitive industry bidding for leases in a competitive market.

The effects of mergers are not reflected in the trends observable in these measures over time. More recent mega-mergers are only reflected in the last two or three years of the data series analyzed, but their effects do not change the quantitative measures of the concentration of the industry or lease market. Comparing major and non-major companies as defined by EIA criteria does not indicate significant differences. Similarly, an analysis of patterns of bidding by those firms on MMS' Restricted Bidders List does not suggest non-competitive behavior, although an analysis of the criteria stipulated for compiling the list raises questions about the list's relevance and rationale.

Effects of mergers were analyzed following two complementary approaches. In the first, leases acquired during the 1983 to 1999 period were divided into groups based upon merger and acquisition experience. Over the entire time period the comparisons indicated that leases acquired by firms without merger and acquisition experience elicited significantly higher bids than those acquired by firms with merger and acquisition experience. However, if the leases were subdivided into those acquired during the 1983 to 1989 period, and those acquired in the 1990 to 1999 period, the differences became insignificant in the later period.

Following the second approach entailed making comparisons between majors and non-majors and between those firms listed on MMS' Restricted Bidders List and those not on the list. These comparisons showed the same pattern of significant differences in the 1983-89 period weakening in the 1990-99 period for the financial variables measuring the average value of bids. However, the structural variables measuring the number of bidders and the number of bids per lease showed consistent, significantly lower, values for restricted bidders in both time periods.

Econometric analyses were also applied to data on lease sales in the U.S. Gulf of Mexico OCS region in order to incorporate other relevant factors into the analysis. The same two approaches were followed. In the first, regression equations were estimated for each of the groups of leases, referred to previously, to identify potential effects of mergers and acquisitions on the mean value of high bonus bids, along with other hypothesized determinants, such as: intensity of competition, extent of competition, type of bid, lease location/water depth, economic conditions, and structural changes in the E&P industry. A Wald coefficient restriction test was applied to the regression results to ascertain differences in coefficients in the equations.

The parameters designated as fixed effects (intercepts) were significantly different in magnitude among the groups. The differences suggest that the relative change in the mean value of high bonus bids for OCS leases, *ceteris paribus*, was relatively smaller for leases in which participating bidders include a firm or firms with M&A experience during the period 1983-1999, when other factors have been accounted for.

This result could be interpreted either as suggesting these firms were able to exercise some degree of oligopsony power, or as suggesting that they possessed better information or had more leasing experience, which enabled them to bid more efficiently. Since measures of competition were not significantly different, the second option seems more plausible.

In the second approach, a set of interactive dummy variables was employed to define eight combinations of: 1) type of bid (joint or solo), 2) existence and extent of competition (ex post) [1] in bidding, and 3) firm size, (using the major/non major or the restricted bidder/unrestricted bidder classifications as proxies for firm size). Merger and acquisition experience was included in the regression equation and had the same significant, negative relationship as in the first model.

In general, both econometric approaches led to findings that are consistent with other studies and theoretical expectations. Both also show that as ex post competition increases, the average value of the high bonus bids increases and this is true regardless of the mergers and acquisition experience of the participants winning the lease. Similarly, the study shows that joint bidding for leases does not lead to anticompetitive bidding outcomes, again regardless of the M&A status of the bidders. However, taking account of the effects of the other intervening factors that could be expected to affect the value of high bids, the econometric analysis suggests that bidders with M&A experience paid less than bidders without M&A experience for OCS leases.

---

[1] "Ex post competition" is used since the lease sale is a sealed bid auction and bidders do not necessarily know if other operators are bidding on the lease. They may have such information, however, from other sources.

# TABLE OF CONTENTS

Page

List of Figures ................................................................................................ ix

List of Tables ................................................................................................. xi

Executive Summary ........................................................................................ 1

Section 1    Introduction ............................................................................. 17

Section 2    OCS Lease Market Structure, Conduct and Performance ...... 19
            2.1 Background on OCS Leasing ........................................... 19
            2.2 Competitive Structure of the Market for OCS Leases ...... 20
            2.3 Bidding Arrangements for OCS Leases ........................... 32
            2.4 Characterizing the Market for OCS Leases ..................... 34

Section 3    Mergers and Acquisitions, Firm Size and the Market for OCS Leases ...... 47
            3.1 Effects of Mergers and Acquisitions. ............................. 47
            3.2 Comparing the Lease Records of Majors and Non-Majors ...... 53
            3.3 The Restricted Joint Bidders and OCS Lease Market ...... 58
            3.4 Conclusions .................................................................... 68

Section 4    Econometric Analysis of the Market for OCS Leases ............. 69
            4.1 Model Specification ....................................................... 69
            4.2 Model Estimation and Regression Results ...................... 72
            4.3 Effects of Mergers and Acquisitions on the Value of OCS Leases ...... 75
            4.4 Firms of Different Sizes and the Value of OCS Leases ...... 77

Section 5    Conclusions and Implications ................................................. 84

Section 6    References ............................................................................. 85

# LIST OF FIGURES

| Figure | Description | Page |
|---|---|---|
| ES1 | Herfindahl Indices of Industry Competitiveness | 3 |
| ES2 | Z-Scores for Average Bids (All Bids) | 5 |
| 2.1 | Annual Oil and Gas Production by Firms from the Gulf of Mexico OCS Measured in MMBarrels of Oil Equivalent, 1947-2001 | 21 |
| 2.2 | Cumulative Oil and Gas Production by Firms from the Gulf of Mexico OCS Measured in MMBarrels of Oil Equivalent, 1947-2001 | 21 |
| 2.3 | Share of Production from the U.S. GOM, U.S. and the World for the Top 50 Firms Operating in the U.S. Gulf of Mexico OCS | 27 |
| 2.4 | Average Number of Bids Per Lease in Different Periods | 32 |
| 2.5 | Trend in the Value of the High Bonus Bids, 1983-1999 | 35 |
| 2.6 | Trend in the Index of the Annual Average Value of High Bids | 36 |
| 2.7 | Z-Scores for Average High Bids (Shallow Water) | 41 |
| 2.8 | Z-Scores for Average High Bids (Deep Water) | 42 |
| 2.9 | Z-Scores for Average High Bids (Competitive Bids) | 43 |
| 2.10 | Z-Scores for Average High Bids (Single Bids) | 44 |
| 2.11 | Z-Scores for Average High Bids (All Bids) | 45 |
| 3.1 | Percent Decline in Aggregate Lease Market Performance Attributes Between the 1980s and 1990s | 57 |
| 3.2 | Percent Decline in Average High Bonus Bids by Lease Structure and Conduct Between the 1980s and 1990s | 57 |
| 3.3 | Share of GOM Production by MMS' Restricted Joint Bidders, 1982-2000 | 61 |
| 3.4 | Total Production for MMS' Restricted Bidders in the GOM, 1983-2000 | 61 |
| 3.5 | Percent of JV High Bids and JV Bonuses for MMS' Restricted Bidders, 1983-2000 | 63 |
| 3.6 | Location of Texaco/Chevron's Joint Bids, 1996-1999 | 66 |

# LIST OF TABLES

| Table | Description | Page |
|---|---|---|
| ES1 | Measures of the Competitive Structure, Type of Bid and Value of Mean High Bids for OCS Oil and Gas Leases by Lease Category Groups A and B, 1983-1989 and 1990-1999 | 7 |
| ES2 | Comparison of OCS Lease Sales by Context, Outcome, and Period for Majors and Non-Majors | 8 |
| ES3 | Bidding by Context, Outcome and Period for Leases Won by Restricted and Non-Restricted Bidders | 11 |
| 2.1 | Measures of Competitiveness Based on Leases Acquired, 1983 to 1999 | 23 |
| 2.2 | Measures of Competitiveness Based on Production in the Gulf of Mexico OCS | 25 |
| 2.3 | Gulf of Mexico (GOM) Production and Leases, U.S. Production and Global Production for the Top 50 Firms in Either GOM Production or Leases, 1990 to 1999 | 26 |
| 2.4 | Concentration Ratios, HHI Indices and Total Production for U.S. & GOM | 29 |
| 2.5 | Share of Leases Acquired by Top 4, 8, and 20 Producing Firms | 29 |
| 2.6 | Top 20 Firms in Total Oil and Gas Production or Total Leases Acquired in the Gulf of Mexico, 1990-1999 | 30 |
| 2.7 | Measures of the Intensity of Competition for OCS Leases | 31 |
| 2.8 | Percentage Frequency Distribution of Leases by the Number of Bids | 33 |
| 2.9 | Percent Share of Bids that Were Joint Venture Bids | 34 |
| 2.10 | Average Value of High Bonus Bids, 1983 to 1999 ($000) | 36 |
| 2.11 | Top Twenty Firms in Total Oil and Gas Production or Total Leases Acquired, Average High Bid/Lease for Total, Shallow, Deep, Competitive and Non-Competitive Leases, 1990-1999 | 38 |
| 2.12 | Top Fifty Firms in Either Production or Leases Acquired from 1990 to 1999 Ranked by Z-Scores for Average High Bids, with Z-Scores for Total, Shallow, Deep, Competitive, and Non-Competitive Average High Bids | 39 |
| 3.1 | Aggregate Values of OCS Lease Attributes | 48 |
| 3.2 | Measures of the Competitive Structure, Type of Bid and Value of Mean High Bids for OCS Oil and Gas Leases by Lease Category Groups A, B and C, 1983-1999 | 50 |
| 3.3 | Measures of the Competitive Structure, Type of Bid and Value of Mean High Bids for OCS Oil and Gas Leases by Lease Category Groups A and B, 1983-1989 and 1990-1999 | 51 |
| 3.4 | Frequency Distribution of Bidding by Joint Venturing | 52 |
| 3.5 | Mean Value of High Bids by Structure, Conduct and Lease Category ($ Million) | 53 |
| 3.6 | Comparison of OCS Lease Attributes by Structure and Conduct, 1983-1999 | 54 |
| 3.7 | Comparison of OCS Lease Attributes by Structure, Conduct, and Period | 56 |
| 3.8 | List of Restricted Joint Bidders 1982-2001: Category and Share of Total Gulf of Mexico Production | 59 |
| 3.9 | Number of High Joint Bids by Firms on the Restricted Bidders List and Other Firms: 1983 to 1999 | 63 |
| 3.10 | Lease Attributes for Restricted and Unrestricted Bidders | 67 |

# LIST OF TABLES (continued)

| Table | Description | Page |
|-------|-------------|------|
| 4.1 | Variable Definitions and Hypothesized Signs of the Parameters | 73 |
| 4.2 | Estimated Model of the Value of High Bonus Bids on the Gulf OCS, 1983-99 | 73 |
| 4.3 | Estimated Model of the Value of High Bonus Bids with Coefficient Restrictions | 76 |
| 4.4 | Estimated CAT Model of the Relative Change in the Value of High Bonus Bids with NMSN as the Base Case | 79 |
| 4.5 | Estimated Model of the Relative Change in the Value of High Bonus Bids with Varying Base Case | 79 |
| 4.6 | Estimated CAT Model of the Relative Change in the Value of High Bonus Bids with USN as the Base Case | 82 |
| 4.7 | Estimated Model of the Relative Change in the Value of High Bonus Bids with Varying Base Case | 83 |

# EXECUTIVE SUMMARY

Mergers, acquisitions and other arrangements to achieve control, cooperation, or coordination have characterized the petroleum industry almost from the time that kerosene replaced whale oil as the primary fuel for illumination. During the past decade, most of the largest petroleum companies operating in the United States have joined in "mega-mergers." Large independents active in the Gulf of Mexico as well as many smaller independents also merged.

Regulatory authorities have analyzed the possible effects of each merger and ordered divestitures or other arrangements where the new organization threatened competition or other desirable economic attributes or ends. The regulators' attention has been focused on retail or wholesale markets for petroleum products, although on the west coast impacts on refinery inputs have also been a source of concern.

The focus of this study is different. Our interest is the possible effects of mergers and acquisitions on the U.S. Treasury as the recipient of royalties and bonuses paid by companies to explore for and produce oil and gas from reserves on the Outer Continental Shelf (OCS).

**Data and Methods:** Descriptive and econometric analyses were applied to data on lease sales in the U.S. Gulf of Mexico OCS region during the period 1983-1999. The analyses were limited to 1983-1999 to correspond to the period since the area-wide leasing policy began. The study's unit of analysis is primarily the sale of each lease with the participants in, or bidders for, the lease divided into different groups. For some analyses, leases are divided into three groups depending on whether the firm or group of firms submitting the winning bid included:

1) Firms with merger and acquisition experience at the time of the bid,
2) Firms who would be involved in mergers or acquisitions in the future, or
3) Firms who were without such experience during the study period.

Comparisons were made to see if there were significant differences among the three groups, and this grouping was also used in econometric analyses.

A supplementary set of analyses focusing on firm-size was conducted with leases classified by: 1) whether the winning bid included firms classified as "majors/non-majors" by the Energy Information Agency (EIA), and 2) whether the winning bid included firms named on the Restricted Bidders List that MMS is required to publish twice a year.

Leases also were classified into eight categories based on firm size, bidding strategy and lease structure. The second and third chapters of the study are a descriptive analysis of the data that included tests for the significance of differences in the mean value of some lease attributes. The fourth chapter is an econometric analysis of high or winning bonus bids that incorporates other relevant factors in the analysis.

**Industry Characteristics and Background:** Annual and cumulative production since offshore development began in the late 1940s reveal important elements of both stability and change.

- Chevron, Shell, Exxon, Mobil, and Texaco who are leading oil and gas producers in the Gulf of Mexico today, and are responsible for a correspondingly substantial share of cumulative production, provide the stability.

- But comparing annual and cumulative production also reveals significant changes in the offshore industry. For example:
  - BP is a top-five producer today, but as a relative newcomer to the Gulf of Mexico still ranks only 23rd in cumulative production.
  - Conoco, an offshore pioneer, ranks 26th in annual production but still is among the top-five in cumulative production.
  - Eight of today's top-30 annual producers have not produced enough to be ranked amongst the top-30 cumulative producers.
  - In 1980 the combined production by all non-top-30 producers ranked 16th in terms of annual production. Today the combined group ranks second.

Mergers, acquisitions, divestitures, changing corporate strategies, good and bad investment decisions, technological innovation, international politics, global economics and luck are reflected in these changes, but the data indicate a history of substantial change in internal organizational as well as external circumstances.

**Measuring Concentration and Competition:** An after-the-fact-indicator of competition is the extent to which leases are concentrated. If leases are won or held by only a few firms, the implication is that competition in lease sales has been less effective or intense than if leases were distributed more broadly. An issue raised in our study is whether concentration should be measured directly by the distribution of leases acquired, or indirectly by the share of production accounted for by the firms bidding for leases. And, if production is used, should it be production in the Gulf of Mexico, in the U.S., or global production.

The most comprehensive and commonly used measure of concentration is the Herfindahl Index (HHI) that measures both the absolute and the relative concentration of the market shares. The HHI is defined as the sum of the squares of the market shares of all participating firms in the lease auction market in a given period or year—considering the size of all participants, not just the largest four or largest eight.

Industry or market concentration often is broadly characterized using the magnitude of the HHI index. A market that has HHI of less than 1,000 is less concentrated and can be described as being competitive. Dougher (1987) argues that a market is moderately concentrated if its HHI lies between 1,000 and 1,800, or highly concentrated when its HHI is greater than 1,800.

**Figure ES1** shows the HHI for the decade of the 1990s calculated with three different bases: leases acquired, production in the Gulf of Mexico OCS, and total U.S. production. All three indices are well below the 1000 minimal value for a "concentrated" designation, throughout the period.

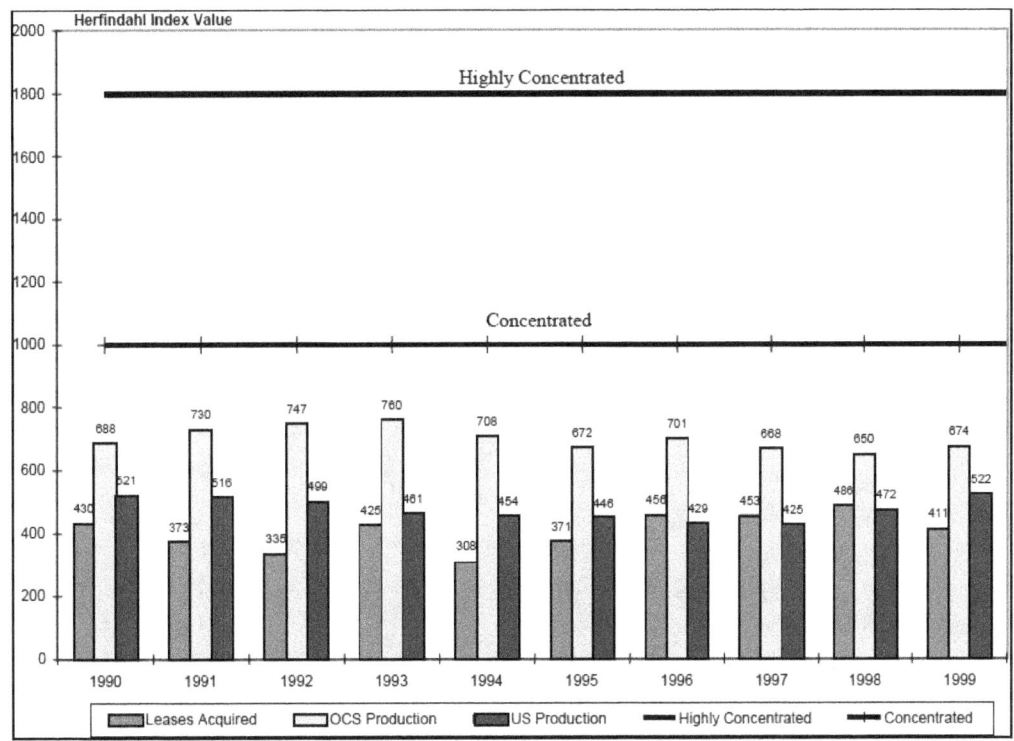

Figure ES1: Herfindahl Indices of Industry Competitiveness.

Leases are held for varying terms. Some are turned back after their initial 5-year term; others are held as long as there is production or related activity on the lease, such as pumping. Thus the stock or inventory of active leases that a firm controls will differ from the number of leases it acquires. The HHI for active leases held is 406, which is reasonably close to the average HHI based on leases acquired during the 1990 to 1999 period of 307, and well below the 1,000 mark of a concentrated industry.

Competition measured in terms of bids per lease on the OCS, on average, appears to be significantly less intense during the period 1983-1999 compared to earlier history. A similar decline has occurred in the proportion of bids submitted as joint ventures of two or more firms, and as the proportion of bids by joint ventures declined through time, the proportion of high bonus bids awarded to joint venture bidders also declined.

Although traditional measures, regardless of the base used, indicate the industry is well below levels conventionally used to define a concentrated industry, direct measures of participation in bidding indicate less intensity in the competition for leases than in early periods.

***The Value of High Bonus Bids:*** The value of high bonus bids provides a measure of the initial cash payment to the government for granting firms the right to explore in the OCS. As such it is an important variable to monitor and understand. Consistently, the data show higher bonus bids for competitive leases than for noncompetitive leases, irrespective of the type of bid.

- When leases were won through competitive joint venture bidding, the average value of

3

the high bonus bid per lease was $3.29 million, more than twice the value of noncompetitive, joint venture, high bonus bids, which was $1.18 million.

- The average high bonus bid for competitive solo venture bids for the period 1983-1999 was $1.75 million in comparison to an average high bid value of $0.614 million for noncompetitive solo ventures.

There is also considerable variation among average bids by firms, especially at the extremes of the distributions. For all bids, the average ranges from Marathon's high of $1,418,000 to a low of $186,000 for Zilkha—a ratio of 7.6:1. Neither of these firms were small or marginal participants in the lease market. Marathon ranked 10th in production and 18th in leases acquired while Zilkha was the sixth highest in terms of leases and 37th in production. It might be expected that the variation would narrow if leases were subdivided into shallow/deep and competitive/noncompetitive categories, but the high/low and standard deviation/mean ratios actually increase.

Corporate strategy, experience, development strategy and objectives, and a host of other factors are related to the differences in average high bids among the firms listed in the table. Identifying and incorporating such factors into our analysis in a comprehensive way exceeds the scope of this project. However, we try to facilitate the comparison of patterns in bidding results among firms by showing the normalized standard deviation or "Z-score" for each of the average high bid series, as are illustrated in **Figure ES2.**

The Z-score was calculated for the top 50 firms in *either* leases or production, resulting in a sample of 63 firms. A Z-score of zero means the average high bid for the firm lies on the average of all the firms in the distribution, a Z-score of + 1.00 means the firm's average was one standard deviation above the mean of the distribution, a –1.87 means the firm's average was 1.87 standard deviations below the mean of the distribution.

The number of firms that appear to bid either higher or lower than the norm is relatively small.

- Keeping in mind that all the observations are winning bids, "high-winning bids," i.e. bids that are significantly higher than the average winning bid, might suggest worse than average bidding ("worse" from the perspective of the shareholders of the bidders but "better" for the government's revenues) and are referred to here as "too-high-winning bids."

- Six firms, Marathon, Anadarko, Statoil, Elf, Oxy, and Kerr-McGee, might be termed "too-high-winning" bidders and one firm, Zilkha, a "too-low-winning" bidder for all leases considered together.

- The firms listed on MMS' Restricted Bidders List, all fall in the lower end of each of the five bid categories calculated, but only Mobil was (barely) more than one standard deviation below the mean in any series.

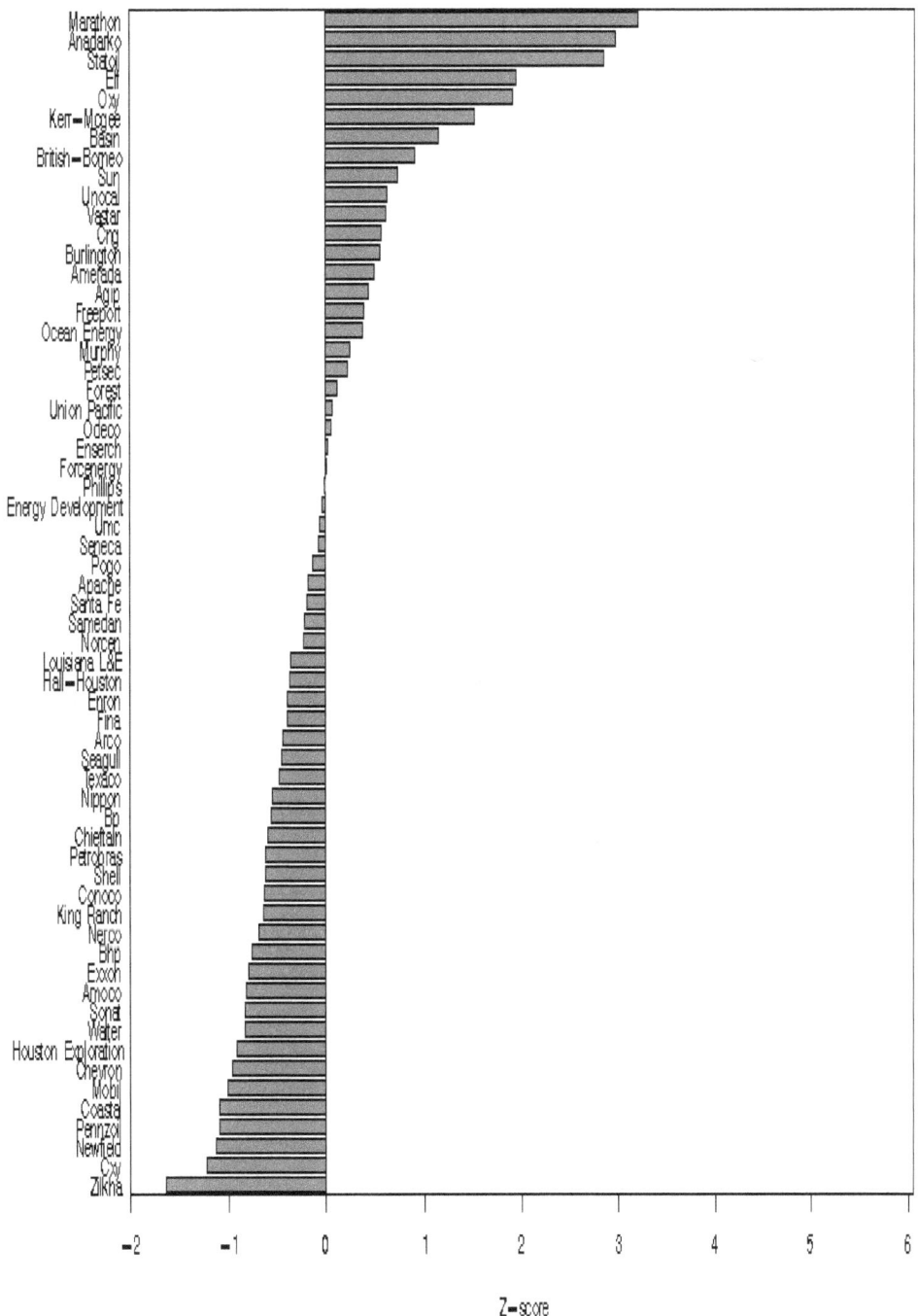

Figure ES2: Z-Scores for Average Bids (All Bids).

*Effects of Mergers and Acquisitions:* To explore the effects of mergers and acquisitions on the value of bids, all OCS leases from 1989-1999 were classified into three categories.

> Group A: Leases with high bids (solo or joint) by firms that were not involved in mergers and acquisitions from 1983-1999. This represented a control group in the analysis.

> Group B: Leases won by firms involved in mergers and acquisitions prior to the time of lease sales during the period 1983-1999. Joint ventures leases, which involved other firms without such experience, were also included in this category.

> Group C: Leases with winning bids submitted solely or jointly by firms that were candidates for mergers and acquisitions ("M&A") between 1983-1999, but M&A had not occurred prior to the time of lease sales. As with Group B, joint ventures leases, which involved firms from Group A, were included.

Differences in the values of variables that describe the context and outcome of the bidding among Groups A and B are described in **Table ES1**, with statistically significant differences indicated in bold type.

The pattern apparent in **Table ES1** is that bids per lease and bidders per lease variables show little consistent, significant difference in either period between Group A and Group B leases. However the financial variables measuring the average value of the high bid and the average amount of "money left on the table," are consistently and significantly larger for the control group (Group A) than for the merger and acquisition group (Group B) in the earlier 1983 to1989 period. But, the differences between Group A and Group B shrink to statistical insignificance in the later 1990 to 1999 period.

*Size of Firms and Lease Values:* Implicit in the concern about possible effects of mergers and acquisitions on the leasing of oil and gas tracts in the Gulf of Mexico is the apprehension that firms participating in the process, thereby, may become large enough to exercise market power for their own advantage. Two groupings based on firm size are used to evaluate this concern— the major/non-major classification used by EIA and the Restricted Bidders List published by MMS.

*Majors/Non-Majors:* **Table ES2** follows the same format and conventions used in **Table ES1**, but it compares the bidding context and outcome for majors and non-majors as defined by the EIA.

Contextual variables are significantly lower for majors than non-majors in both periods. Differences in the average value of the high bid are less prevalent and are mixed in direction. The previous generalization that little if any differences between the groups exist in outcomes in the 1990 to 1999 period appears to apply more strongly.

## Table ES1

### Measures of the Competitive Structure, Type of Bid and Value of Mean High Bids for OCS Oil and Gas Leases by Lease Category Groups A and B, 1983-1989 and 1990-1999

| Variable | Structure | Type of Bid | 1983-1989 Group A[a] | 1983-1989 Group B | 1990-1999 Group A | 1990-1999 Group B |
|---|---|---|---|---|---|---|
| Bids/Lease | Competitive | Joint | 2.78 | 3.00 | 2.78 | 2.86 |
| | | Solo | 2.54 | 2.82 | 2.71 | 2.56 |
| | | All | 2.65 | 2.84 | 2.73 | 2.71 |
| | Aggregate | Joint | 1.60 | 1.47 | 1.66 | 1.56 |
| | | Solo | 1.34 | 1.47 | 1.44(+) | 1.27 |
| | | All | 1.43 | 1.47 | 1.49 | 1.38 |
| Bidders/Lease | Noncompetitive | Joint | 2.60(-) | 3.23 | 2.25 | 2.27 |
| | | All | 1.52(+) | 1.27 | 1.28(-) | 1.42 |
| | Competitive | Joint | 6.09 | 6.00 | 4.85 | 4.73 |
| | | Solo | 3.65 | 3.24 | 3.39 | 3.18 |
| | | All | 4.80(+) | 3.54 | 3.87 | 3.95 |
| | Aggregate | Joint | 3.78 | 3.88 | 3.21(+) | 3.01 |
| | | Solo | 1.58 | 1.58 | 1.61 | 1.38 |
| | | All | 2.38(+) | 1.85 | 2.01 | 1.98 |
| MLOT/Lease, $000 | Competitive[b] | Joint | 2,410(+) | 831 | 942 | 999 |
| | | Solo | 1,520(+) | 666 | 705 | 623 |
| | | All | 1,940(+) | 684 | 784 | 809 |
| High Bids/Lease, $000 | Noncompetitive | Joint | 1,710(+) | 448 | 635 | 551 |
| | | Solo | 974(+) | 396 | 393(+) | 293 |
| | | All | 1,210(+) | 402 | 446 | 378 |
| | Competitive | Joint | 4,500(+) | 1,550 | 1,650 | 1,750 |
| | | Solo | 2,690(+) | 1,190 | 1,240 | 1,120 |
| | | All | 3,540(+) | 1,230 | 1,370 | 1,430 |
| | Aggregate | Joint | 2,660(+) | 708 | 1,010 | 909 |
| | | Solo | 1,350(+) | 602 | 608(+) | 439 |
| | | All | 1,830(+) | 614 | 710 | 610 |

[a]Differences significant at the .95 level for values for Group A and Group B leases are indicated with bold typeface, (+) indicates the value for A is significantly larger and (-) indicating significantly smaller, regular typeface indicates no difference between values for the two groups.

[b] At least two bids are required for any "money to be left on the table."

Table ES2

Comparison of OCS Lease Sales by Context, Outcome, and Period[a] for Majors and Non-Majors

| Variable | Structure | Conduct | 1983-1989 | | 1990-1999 | |
|---|---|---|---|---|---|---|
| | | | Majors | Non-Majors | Majors | Non-Majors |
| Bids/lease | Competitive | Joint | 2.46$^{(-)}$ | 2.83 | 2.66 | 2.82 |
| | | Solo | 2.50 | 2.64 | 2.67 | 2.74 |
| | | All | 2.50$^{(-)}$ | 2.73 | 2.66 | 2.77 |
| | Aggregate | Joint | 1.51 | 1.60 | 1.49$^{(-)}$ | 1.82 |
| | | Solo | 1.32 | 1.39 | 1.38$^{(-)}$ | 1.47 |
| | | All | 1.34$^{(-)}$ | 1.47 | 1.39$^{(-)}$ | 1.57 |
| Bidders/Lease | Noncompetitive | Joint | 2.07$^{(-)}$ | 2.78 | 2.09$^{(-)}$ | 2.45 |
| | | All | 1.09$^{(-)}$ | 1.66 | 1.15$^{(-)}$ | 1.35 |
| | Competitive | Joint | 4.65$^{(-)}$ | 6.01 | 4.53$^{(-)}$ | 5.06 |
| | | Solo | 3.57 | 3.88 | 3.36 | 3.37 |
| | | All | 3.74$^{(-)}$ | 4.91 | 3.58$^{(-)}$ | 4.06 |
| | Aggregate | Joint | 2.97$^{(-)}$ | 3.84 | 2.82$^{(-)}$ | 3.62 |
| | | Solo | 1.55 | 1.68 | 1.53$^{(-)}$ | 1.64 |
| | | All | 1.69$^{(-)}$ | 2.55 | 1.73$^{(-)}$ | 2.23 |
| MLOT/Lease, $000 | Competitive | Joint | 2,073 | 1,647 | 997 | 837 |
| | | Solo | 1,728$^{(+)}$ | 1,172 | 767$^{(+)}$ | 607 |
| | | All | 1,780 | 1,401 | 810 | 702 |
| High Bonus/Lease, $000 | Noncompetitive | Joint | 1,344 | 1,364 | 587 | 676 |
| | | Solo | 907$^{(-)}$ | 1,224 | 419$^{(+)}$ | 325 |
| | | All | 944$^{(-)}$ | 1,276 | 442 | 410 |
| | Competitive | Joint | 3,825 | 3,389 | 1,553 | 1,592 |
| | | Solo | 2,957$^{(+)}$ | 2,292 | 1,300 | 1,137 |
| | | All | 3,090 | 2,822 | 1,348 | 1,324 |
| | Aggregate | Joint | 2,208 | 2,026 | 875 | 1,088 |
| | | Solo | 1,342 | 1,475 | 619 | 545 |
| | | All | 1,428$^{(+)}$ | 1,696 | 657 | 705 |

[a] Significant differences in lease attributes at 95 percent level for leases involving any major firm are indicated accordingly in the table using (+) or (-) superscripted signs. (+) indicates the mean value for majors is significantly larger and (-) indicates the value is significantly smaller than the mean value for leases involving non-majors only.

***Restricted Joint Bidders List:*** The principal MMS policy or regulation intended to promote competition (or inhibit collusion) in the lease market is the Restricted Joint Bidders List. Companies whose global petroleum production is in excess of 1.6 million barrels of oil equivalent per day are listed and prohibited from submitting bids jointly in OCS lease sales.[1]

---

[1] The Act, apparently, does not prohibit firms on list from joint operations, only joint bidding. If a firm on the list wants to acquire a share of a lease which is owned or partly owned by another firm also on the list, it makes a request to MMS to do so which MMS forwards to the U.S. Department of Justice for review. According to MMS personnel, such requests are neither very frequent nor extremely rare occurrences, yet few are denied.

Using global production to determine who the restricted bidders will be, results in a different list than if production in the Gulf of Mexico were to be used. Texaco, for example, dropped off the list in 1989 apparently because its global production fell below the 1.6 million barrel floor. However, in the Gulf of Mexico, Texaco's production was three or four times as large as British Petroleum's, which appeared on the list beginning in 1988. Similarly, Conoco, which is the fourth largest cumulative producer in the Gulf, and was a top-5 producer during the 1970s and 1980s, never has been listed as a restricted bidder.

The effects of the mergers can be clearly seen.

- Before the merger, BP's share had been growing steadily, but after its merger with Amoco it jumped from 5.2 to 7.8 percent in 1999.

- When BP acquired ARCO and its E&P subsidiary Vastar, BP's share increased to 10.5 percent making it the second largest producer in the Gulf.

- Exxon and Mobil both experienced declining production shares prior to their merger, and the post merger increase for Exxon/Mobil was more modest—4.1 percent to 7 percent.

Although changes in production shares of this magnitude warrant analysis, and it seems paradoxical that the prohibition against joint bidding does not appear to have been a factor considered in the review of the mergers among firms appearing on the list, it is important to keep an accurate sense of scale. In a relative sense, changes in the shares of BP/Amoco/Vastar and Exxon/Mobil are dominated by the near doubling of Shell's share from about 11.5 to 21.2 percent over the period. As Shell's share of Gulf production nearly doubled, its absolute production increased from 120.796 to 292.129 million barrels. Previous to their mergers, the production levels of the other restricted bidders were stable or were declining. Thus, both of the major mergers observable resulted in much less concentration of production than did the payoff from non-merger-participant Shell's very successful investment in the deep Gulf.

There are significant differences observable among firms appearing on the List during the 1983 to 1999 study period in their use of joint bidding.

- BP, Exxon and Shell use joint bids less extensively than the average.
  o Only 12.5 percent of BP's high bids were made jointly and bonuses paid with those bids amounted to less than 10 percent of BP's total for the period.
  o For Exxon the comparable percentages were about 25 percent for high bids and 19 percent for bonuses paid.
  o Of Shell's market-leading 1,824 high bids only about 15 percent were made jointly and bonuses paid with those bids amounted to about 22 percent of the firm's total.

- Amoco and Texaco are of special interest because they were restricted bidders for relatively short increments of the 1983 to 1999 period--one year for Amoco and six for Texaco. When not on the list they were free to, and did, bid jointly with the firms listed.

- Texaco led the restricted bidder's group in the proportion of joint bids with about 56 percent.
- Amoco was second to Texaco with about 42 percent of its high bids made jointly.
- Although an active joint bidder, Amoco had partnered neither with BP nor Vastar prior to their merger.

- Texaco and Chevron, in contrast to BP and Amoco, had an extensive record of joint bidding that closely preceded their merger.
    - Texaco, prior to their merger, cooperated with Chevron in 163 joint bids, of which 136 were winning bids. This amounted to about 28 percent of Texaco's total of 493 joint winning bids.
    - Further, all of the joint Texaco/Chevron bids took place in the last four years of the study period with 158 of the 163 bids submitted during the three sales held in 1996 and 1997.

Many considerations of technology, strategy and corporate planning, globally as well as in the Gulf of Mexico, may have influenced the Chevron/Texaco merger decision, but this episode of collaboration is notable.

An extensive analysis of joint bidding by the two firms is beyond the scope of the study, but the context in which it took place is important. In 1995 there were 1,012 leases in water depth of 800 meters or more in effect. In 1996 that number increased to 1,491 and in 1997 to 3,002—a nearly three-fold increase. Further, by 2001, deepwater-leases had only increased to 3,424 (Baud, et al., 2002:14) Thus, a desire to broaden their participation in this "leasing-up" of the deepwater Gulf, may have been a factor in Chevron/Texaco joint-bidding offensive. There also may have been elements of "catch-up" or "keep-up" involved.

**Table ES3**, following the same format and conventions of the previous two tables, compares the bidding context and outcomes for leases won by restricted bidders, (or joint bids including restricted bidders) with other leases.

- A pattern of fewer bids per lease and fewer bidders per lease for leases won by restricted bidders is evident over the entire period and becomes more pervasive in the later 1990 to 1999 period.

- For the outcome variables, in the earlier period three of the significant differences are positive and three are negative. In the latter period, there are also six significantly different categories but all of them are negative.

Table ES3

Bidding by Context, Outcome and Period for Leases Won by Restricted and Nonrestricted Bidders[a]

| Variable | Structure | Conduct | 1983-1989 | | 1990-1999 | | 1983-1999 | |
|---|---|---|---|---|---|---|---|---|
| | | | Restricted | Non-Restricted | Restricted | Non-Restricted | Restricted | Non-Restricted |
| Bids/ Lease | Competitive | Joint | 2.86 | 2.76 | 2.49[(-)] | 2.80 | 2.77 | 2.79 |
| | | Solo | 2.40[(-)] | 2.64 | 2.53[(-)] | 2.75 | 2.47[(-)] | 2.72 |
| | | All | 2.59 | 2.70 | 2.52[(-)] | 2.77 | 2.56[(-)] | 2.75 |
| | Aggregate | Joint | 1.62 | 1.60 | 1.26[(-)] | 1.72 | 1.48[(-)] | 1.67 |
| | | Solo | 1.25[(-)] | 1.41 | 1.29[(-)] | 1.46 | 1.27[(-)] | 1.45 |
| | | All | 1.35[(-)] | 1.49 | 1.29[(-)] | 1.54 | 1.32[(-)] | 1.53 |
| Bidders/ Lease | Non-competitive | Joint | 2.60[(-)] | 2.70 | 2.09[(-)] | 2.31 | 2.38[(-)] | 2.49 |
| | | All | 1.38[(-)] | 1.68 | 1.20[(-)] | 1.34 | 1.29[(-)] | 1.46 |
| | Competitive | Joint | 6.24 | 6.13 | 4.06[(-)] | 4.90 | 5.70 | 5.38 |
| | | Solo | 3.41[(-)] | 3.84 | 3.08[(-)] | 3.45 | 3.24[(-)] | 3.56 |
| | | All | 4.57 | 4.99 | 3.25[(-)] | 4.02 | 3.97[(-)] | 4.35 |
| | Aggregate | Joint | 3.80 | 3.87 | 2.44[(-)] | 3.35 | 3.28[(-)] | 3.58 |
| | | Solo | 1.44[(-)] | 1.72 | 1.40[(-)] | 1.65 | 1.42[(-)] | 1.67 |
| | | All | 2.09[(-)] | 2.64 | 1.58[(-)] | 2.16 | 1.84[(-)] | 2.33 |
| MLOT/ Lease, $000 | Competitive | Joint | 4,705[(+)] | 2,316 | 936 | 923 | 3,773[(+)] | 1,465 |
| | | Solo | 1,650 | 1,483 | 614 | 726 | 1,097 | 946 |
| | | All | 2,897[(+)] | 1,903 | 667 | 804 | 1,899[(+)] | 1,170 |
| High Bonus/ Lease, $000 | Non-competitive | Joint | 2,001 | 1,685 | 332[(-)] | 691 | 1,280 | 1,140 |
| | | Solo | 807[(-)] | 1,187 | 385 | 385 | 589 | 629 |
| | | All | 1,090[(-)] | 1,385 | 376[(-)] | 464 | 733 | 786 |
| | Competitive | Joint | 7,567[(+)] | 4,301 | 1,357 | 1,646 | 6,032[(+)] | 2,679 |
| | | Solo | 2,763 | 2,729 | 1,090 | 1,274 | 1,871 | 1,697 |
| | | All | 4,725[(+)] | 3,522 | 1,134[(-)] | 1,421 | 3,117[(+)] | 2,121 |
| | Aggregate | Joint | 3,844[(+)] | 2,579 | 513[(-)] | 1,074 | 2,572[(+)] | 1,719 |
| | | Solo | 1,164[(-)] | 1,575 | 520[(-)] | 620 | 828 | 907 |
| | | All | 1,901 | 2,005 | 519[(-)] | 757 | 1,224 | 1,187 |

[a] Significant differences in lease attributes at 95 percent level for leases involving any restricted bidder are indicated in the table using (+) or (-) superscripted signs. A (+) indicates the mean value for restricted is significantly larger and a (-) that the value is significantly smaller than the mean value for leases involving unrestricted only.

- This result is consistent with the argument that the leases won by the large firms on the Restricted Bidders List, were subject to fewer bids by fewer bidders and were won by significantly lower bids than leases won by firms that did not include restricted bidders.

- This conclusion does not account for other factors that may influence lease values, which are addressed in the econometric analyses reported in **Table ES3**.

The iterative seemingly unrelated regression (SUR) procedure in the QMS Eviews program (version 4.0) was applied to the data to estimate a log-linear specification of the relationship between lease value and its determinants. The log-linear specification yields parameter estimates that are interpretable as the relative change in the dependent variable with respect to an absolute change in the independent variable. In general, the model is consistent with or "explains" about 50 percent of the expected variation in the relative value of high bonus bids as indicated by the $R^2$ statistics. Conversely, by implication, there are other variables not included in this model that may "explain" another 50 percent of the variation expected in the relative magnitude of high bonus bids.

***Econometric Modeling of the Value of Leases:*** We made use of two simple econometric-model frameworks to explore the patterns and trends in the value of OCS leases. The first model estimates the relationship between the value of leases and postulated explanatory factors by using each of the merger and acquisition (M&A) experience categories (Groups A, B, and C, discussed previously) to estimate separate regression equations with coefficients measuring their influence on bidding. Statistical tests then are applied to see which factors consistently influence the value of high bids on the three groups of leases. The second model or approach uses a "major/non-major" or "restricted bidder/nonrestricted bidder" delineation as proxies for firm size with combinations of type of bid and existence of bidding competition as eight separate interactive variables, which are combined with merger and acquisition history or experience and other explanatory variables in the regression equation.

Both approaches are derivative of the same basic conceptual framework, which specifies that the value of the high or winning bonus bid (HB) is a function of three sets of factors: economics, structure, and conduct. This specification has been used successfully several times in the past to analyze lease auction market performance.

In general, the econometric results confirm the following expectations:

- Greater competition is associated with higher mean values of high bonus bids. As competition increases, the relative change in the mean value of high bonus bids will increase.

- The economic environment measured in terms of the rising crude petroleum prices does not lead to a significantly higher mean value of high bids for most leases as would have been expected. However, another measure of perceptions of the economic environment, the carry-over effects of the collapse of crude oil prices in 1986 which brought about major strategic and structural changes in the global E&P industry, does consistently indicate a significant reduction in the mean value of high bonus bids for leases in comparison to the pre-1986 mean value of high bids.

- The mean value of high bonus bids for leases with at least two bids (competitive) is greater than the mean value of single-bid leases (noncompetitive).

- The mean value of high bonus bids for deepwater leases is significantly higher than shallow water leases.

- Joint venturing is associated significantly with higher winning bonus bids than is the case for bids by solo ventures.

To decipher and analyze the potential effects of merger and acquisitions on the mean value of high bonus bids through its determinants--intensity of competition, extent of competition, type of bid, lease location/water depth, economics, and structural changes in the E&P industry, a Wald coefficient restriction test was applied to the regression to ascertain whether the coefficients measuring the relationship between the explanatory variables and the average high bid for the three groups are significantly different from one another.
The Wald test results indicated that:

- The intensity of competition for a lease has a positive, strong, and significant effect on the magnitude of the winning bid, but it is not affected by M&A experience, i.e., it affects all three groups to the same degree.

- As with the intensity of competition variable, the relationship between high bids and whether or not there are competing bidders is strong and significant but the same for all three groups.

- The high bonus bid for deepwater leases over the leases on the shelf is not significantly affected by M&A bidders' participation in the high bonus bid. Again, it affects all three groups to the same degree.

- The involvement of bidders ranking as the top four firms in cumulative production significantly leads to a lower relative value of high bids in the Group B leases. Whereas the expected mean value of high bonus bids for Groups A and C leases involving bidders ranked among the top four is not significantly different from other bidders, i.e., non-top-four bidders.

- The value of high bonus bids has dropped significantly since the collapse of world crude oil prices. The effect is strong in all three groups but is less so for leases in which participating firms had been involved in or would become involved in M&A activities.

- The parameters designated as fixed effects (intercepts) are significantly different in magnitude, thus suggesting that the relative change in the mean value of high bonus bids for OCS leases, *ceteris paribus*, was on average relatively smaller for leases in which participating bidders include a firm or firms involved in M&A, when other factors have been accounted for. This result could be interpreted as suggesting these firms were able to exercise some degree of oligopsony power as a consequence of M&A activities, or as suggesting that this group of firms possessed better information or had more experience, which enabled them to bid more efficiently. Since the competitive measures indicate no significant difference among the three categories, the second interpretation is more consistent with our data.

13

The second econometric formulation or approach is similar to the one used in Mead et al. (1985) in which different possible categories of leases were assembled based on: 1) type of bid (joint or solo), 2) extent or existence of competition in bidding, and 3) firm size, *but using the major/non-major classification as a proxy*. The three categories were used to define a set of interactive dummy variables:

- MJC: High bonus bids which involved major oil and gas operators, bidding jointly for competitive leases (D1).

- MJN: High bonus bids which involved major oil and gas operators, bidding jointly for noncompetitive leases (D2).

- MSC: High bonus bids which involved major oil and gas operators, bidding solo for competitive leases (D3).

- MSN: High bonus bids which involved major oil and gas operators, bidding solo for noncompetitive leases (D4).

- NMJC: High bonus bids involving non-major oil and gas operators only, bidding jointly for competitive leases (D5).

- NMJN: High bonus bids involving non-major oil and gas operators, bidding jointly for noncompetitive leases (D6).

- NMSC: High bonus bids involving non-major oil and gas operators, bidding solo for competitive leases (D7).

- NMSN: High bonus bids involving non-major oil and gas operators, bidding solo for noncompetitive leases.

Given our study objectives, the most relevant results from this study using this approach are:

1) The inverse relationship between *DMA* (M&A history and experience), and the average level of high bids, which supports the previous findings that firms with history of M&A, on average, submit lower winning bids (other factors taken into account) than firms that have not.

2) Comparisons of the differences among coefficients of the interactive dummy variables, D1 through D7, which shows that:

   - All of the interactive dummy variables for majors have larger coefficients than the corresponding combination including only non-majors, i.e., D1 (*MJC*)>D5 (*NMJC*), D2 > D6, D3>D7. However the differences are significant only for solo bids, both those that are competitive and those that are not. This suggests that if firm size, as measured by the major/non-major classification, has any effect on bidding it is a positive effect.

14

- The fact that there is no significant difference between joint bids involving majors and joint bids not involving majors, i.e., *MJC and NMJC, or MJN and NMJN,* supports skepticism about the rationale for the Restricted-Bidders-List approach for discouraging anti-competitive behavior through restrictions on joint-bidding.

- Within both major and non-major classifications, competitive bids are consistently and significantly higher than noncompetitive bids, reinforcing the results of previous sections.

Following the same format and method, but substituting the firms designated by MMS as restricted bidders for the EIA's "major" category and all firms not so designated for the "non-major" category, gives results that are quite similar. This is not surprising since the unit of analysis, or observation, is the individual lease. Although the number of firms designated as restricted bidders is small, they account for a substantial proportion of the leases acquired by the "major" category.

The implications drawn from the analysis based on the major/non-major classification hold for the restricted/unrestricted bidder classification as well.

- Comparisons of the coefficients of the interactive variables for restricted and unrestricted bidders support the previous conclusion that if firm size has any effect on the value of the average high bid, it is a positive one.

- Comparisons of coefficients for joint bidding indicate no significant difference between restricted and unrestricted bidders for both competitive and noncompetitive bids and seem to directly challenge the rationale for the Restricted Bidders List.

The only difference in the parameter estimates between the major/non-major and restricted/unrestricted categories was that the crude oil price index coefficient had a positive sign, as postulated, in the former but a negative sign in the latter case. The post price collapse variable, which we previously suggested was probably a more relevant and direct reflection of perceptions of the economic expectations, however, had the same sign in both categories.

***Summary and Conclusions:*** Neither aggregate measures used to analyze concentrated market and industry structures, nor patterns of joint bidding among firms active in the offshore Gulf of Mexico suggest either a decrease or a deficiency in the competitiveness of the lease sales held by the U.S. Minerals Management Service. Whether leases acquired at the sales, or production by firms bidding for leases, are used as the base of the concentration measures, they indicate a competitive industry bidding for leases in a competitive market.

The effects of mergers are not reflected in the trends observable in these measures over time. More recent mega-mergers are only reflected in the last two or three years of the data series analyzed, but their effects do not change the quantitative measures of the concentration of the industry or lease market. Comparing major and non-major companies as defined by EIA criteria does not indicate significant differences. Similarly, an analysis of patterns of bidding by those firms on MMS' Restricted Bidders List does not suggest noncompetitive behavior, although an analysis of the criteria for compiling it raises questions about the list's relevance and rationale.

More inclusive econometric approaches led to findings that are consistent with other studies and theoretical expectations. As competition (ex post) increases, the average value of the high bonus bids increases, regardless of the mergers and acquisition experience of the participants winning the lease. Similarly, joint bidding for leases does not lead to anticompetitive bidding outcomes, again regardless of the M&A status of the bidders.

However, taking account of the effects of the other intervening factors expected to affect the value of high bids, the econometric analysis suggests that bidders with M&A experience paid less than bidders without M&A experience for OCS leases. In the first econometric approach the size of firms, per se, had a statistically significant negative affect on average lease value only for leases won by firms with M&A experience. When major/non-major or restricted/nonrestricted bidders were used as proxies for firm size the effect was either positive or statistically insignificant.

# 1. Introduction

Over the past century, the structure, composition and organization of the oil and gas industry have changed repeatedly, as have the industry's broader technological, political and economic context and culture. The petroleum industry, as we know it now, was created when Standard Oil was conceived and grew to a near monopoly. Since then, the industry's major transformations include:

- The break-up of Standard Oil by the Anti-trust Division of the U.S. Justice Department;

- The era of controlled or administered prices by the "seven sisters" and the Texas Railroad Commission from the Second World War to the embargo by the Arab Oil Exporting Countries in 1973;

- The rise of the national oil companies in the 1960s and 1970s, and the evolution of transparent and open, if at times cloudy, markets for oil and gas; and,

- The price collapse and subsequent restructuring of the mid-1980s.

Some expect the recent consolidation of most of the largest firms in the industry, the so-called mega-mergers, to result in change and reorganization comparable in magnitude and consequence to these earlier episodes. The wave of mega-mergers is too recent, however, to be able to subject this conjecture to testing with data. Further, concurrently with the mega-mergers, there have been major changes in the industry's external environment. Many petroleum producing countries are trying to entice the international majors, large independents and in some cases their own private domestic companies into participating in the development of reserves that formerly were open only to their national oil and gas companies. Those pursing these strategies include countries previously unfriendly to global capitalism, such as India, Iran, Iraq, Libya, Russia and the other former countries of the Soviet Union. Even in the U.S., the development of the "Deep Gulf of Mexico" in the late 1990s, which was a sea change in the technology and economics of the industry, was led by a non-U.S. firm, Shell, with British Petroleum also a major participant.

Thus, although the new "mega-mergers" have created some of the largest privately owned corporate entities in the world, the rise of national oil companies and other changes in the industry's external environment have diminished the dominance of privately owned, domestic, companies.

Acknowledging these inherent limitations, this study examines empirically some of the possible impacts of corporate consolidation and reorganization on petroleum resource allocation in the Gulf of Mexico OCS region. The study applies theoretical and empirical tools in anti-trust, market and industrial structure, organization and performance to describe the changes that have taken place--especially among firms active in the Gulf of Mexico OCS. The study relies on information on OCS leases including the sale date of each lease, lease number and location, the number of bids submitted, the name of bidders, the dollar value of each bid, the value of the winning bids, drilling and production history, and royalty and rental payments for the right of private firms to explore, develop and produce oil from the OCS.

All OCS leases have been classified into three ownership categories on the basis of whether the high (that is successful or winning) bonus bid was made by a firm involved prior to lease sale in mergers and acquisition activity, or, in the case of joint bids, where at least one bidder had such a history. Winning bids by firms without M&A history formed the second category and bids by firms without "M&A" experience at the time of the bid but were involved in such activity later, made up the third category. The data on leases were also classified into several lease categories on the basis of firm size, bidding arrangement, and bidding structure.

Two other dimensions of the industry's organization were also analyzed. The Minerals Management Service's own Restricted Bidders List was analyzed and comparisons were made between "major" and "independent" or "non-major companies" (where "major" was defined as those included in the Energy Information Administration's Financial Reporting System— essentially companies owning at least one percent of global oil or natural gas reserves or production) in an effort to see how the size of the firm may affect attributes of OCS lease sales.

Two statistical approaches were used. The first approach was a descriptive analysis of the data and the testing of differences in the mean of some lease attributes, which characterize the structure and nature of the lease market, and lease ownership. The other approach was an econometric analysis of the leasing records, specifically, the relationship between the values of high bonus bids and competition, bidding arrangement, industry economics and other variables. The econometric approach allows for the evaluation of the variability of high bids for leases in terms of the perceived quality of the lease or tract, the size of firms bidding, the bidding methods--solo or joint, the location in terms of water depth and state jurisdiction, and firm characteristics.

The report is organized into five sections and an executive summary. The following section presents a brief overview of the changes in the petroleum industry corporate structure, the motivation and objectives of the project as well an overview of the statistical methodology. Section three presents a descriptive analysis of the structure, conduct and of the market for OCS oil and gas leases since area-wide leasing began in 1983. Several attributes of the market for oil and gas leases are presented and analyzed to determine the impacts of mergers and acquisitions on the lease bonus value on the Gulf of Mexico OCS. The fourth section develops, estimates and exercises a regression model describing the relationship between the value of high bonus bids for OCS oil and gas leases to crude petroleum price index, intensity of competition, bidding strategy, geology and other factors. The final section presents the principal conclusions and recommendations for future research areas on oil and gas leasing on the OCS.

## 2. OCS Lease Market Structure, Conduct and Performance

### 2.1 Background on OCS Leasing

The OCS Land Act of 1953, an act of the United States Congress, established the procedure for transferring the right of private firms to explore, develop and produce petroleum resources in the U.S. Gulf of Mexico Outer Continental Shelf (OCS). The transfer mechanism has mostly been by sealed-bid auction conducted periodically by the Minerals Management Service (MMS), an agency of the U.S. Department of the Interior. Initially, under the auction process, firms made cash bonus offers for tracts that were nominated by them. The Land Act gave a mandate to MMS that the transfer of petroleum leases on the Gulf OCS to private firms should either be by the bonus bidding system with a fixed royalty rate or through a royalty bidding system with a fixed bonus payment.

The final decision to award a lease to a firm or firms depends to large extent on whether the value of the high bid exceeds a predetermined reservation price established by MMS for the lease (Gilley and Karels, 1981). Thus, if a lease is awarded, the firm with the highest offer for a nominated tract among all the accepted bids is granted the right to develop the particular lease for an initial cash bonus. The stipulations for annual rental payment for the lease and a fixed royalty rate are also stated at the time of the award (Rockwood, 1983). The firm or firms winning the lease must drill within five years to avoid forfeiting the lease. Rental payments are paid annually until the lease is surrendered or production begins. Royalty payments, a fixed fraction of the revenue from the production area, are made to MMS when production begins. The lease is usually automatically renewed for as long as there is production on the lease (Porter, 1995).

The bidding process described above is called cash bonus bidding. Critics of this bidding process have argued over the years that the large and unconditional upfront cash bonus payments for leases were barriers to entry and anticompetitive. Rockwood (1983) indicates that such arguments persuaded the U.S. Congress to pass amendments to the original OCS Land Act of 1953 in 1978. The amendments led to a provision that at least 20 percent and at most 60 percent of acreage offering must be leased using leasing systems other than the conventional bonus bidding system. That legislation expired in 1983 even as the new leasing policy for OCS leases became effective in April 1983.

The new policy is called area-wide leasing within a planning area and allows firms to bid for any OCS tracts that have not been previously leased (Moody and Kruvant, 1990). Leases that are repossessed or confiscated for lack of activity after five years of the initial sale, in most cases, are also available. The immediate result of this change in policy was a large increase in the number of leases or tracts awarded at each subsequent sale. The average number of tracts awarded increased from about 300 under the nomination process to an average of more than 5000 under the area-wide leasing procedure within the first few sales.

The question of which leasing program maximizes the U.S. government's chances of a fair market value for the right to drill for and produce oil and gas on public lands continues to provoke debate. In the 1980s, several studies analyzed alternative bidding methods for OCS oil and gas leases (Teisberg, 1980; Gilley and Karels, 1981; Rockwood, 1983; Mead and Sorensen, 1980 and

Mead et al., 1985). These studies concluded that the cash bonus bidding system was the most effective means of allocating petroleum resources for exploration and exploitation. The studies, however, were conducted using data on leases obtained from 1954-1977 under the nomination and tract selection arrangement (Saidi and Marsden, 1992), and the structure of the U.S. oil and gas industry has also changed significantly since that time. It has been reported that many small independent oil and gas operators have become active in the Gulf OCS lease sales and development (Iledare et al., 1995). Moreover, the type of bids that can be submitted has also changed. The Energy Policy and Conservation Act (PL 94-163), enacted in December 1975, forbade some of the major oil and gas producers from bidding jointly for leases on the OCS so as to reduce the potential for anti-competitive effects (Millsaps and Ott, 1981).

## 2.2 Competitive Structure of the Market for OCS Leases

Annual and cumulative production by the top-30 operators, in each category, since offshore development began in the late 1940s is depicted in **Figures 2.1 and 2.2**. They indicate important elements of both stability and change as the industry evolved.

- Chevron, Shell, and ExxonMobil, who are leading oil and gas producers in the Gulf of Mexico today, and are responsible for a corresponding substantial share of cumulative production, provide stability.

- But comparing annual and cumulative production also reveals significant changes in the offshore industry. For example:
    o BP is a top-five producer today, but as a relative newcomer to the Gulf of Mexico still ranks only 23$^{rd}$ in cumulative production.
    o Conoco, an offshore pioneer, ranks 26$^{th}$ in annual production but still is among the top-five in cumulative production.
    o Seven of the today's top-30 annual producers have not produced enough to be ranked amongst the top-30 cumulative producers.
    o In 1980 the combined production by all non-top-30 producers ranked 16$^{th}$ in terms of annual production. Today the combined group ranks second.

Mergers, acquisitions, divestitures, changing corporate strategies, good and bad investment decisions, technological innovation, international politics, global economics and luck are reflected in the changes in the industry illustrated, but the extreme ups-and-downs in the annual production series indicate a history of substantial change in internal organizational as well as external circumstances.

Has the nature or intensity of competition among firms for leases and production changed as the offshore industry evolved?

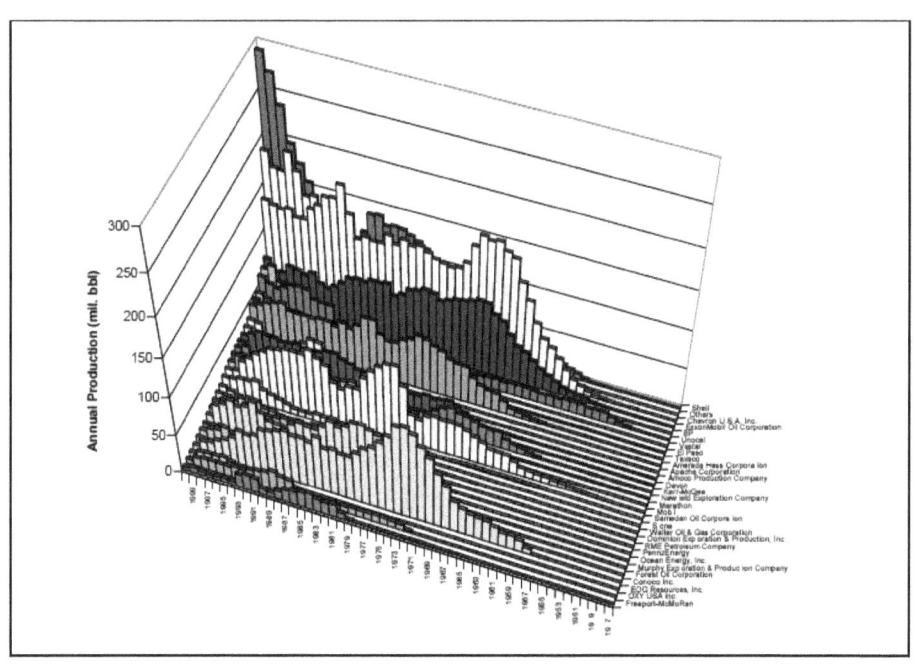

Figure 2.1: Annual Oil and Gas Production by Firms from the Gulf of Mexico OCS
Measured in MMBarrels of Oil Equivalent, 1947-2001.

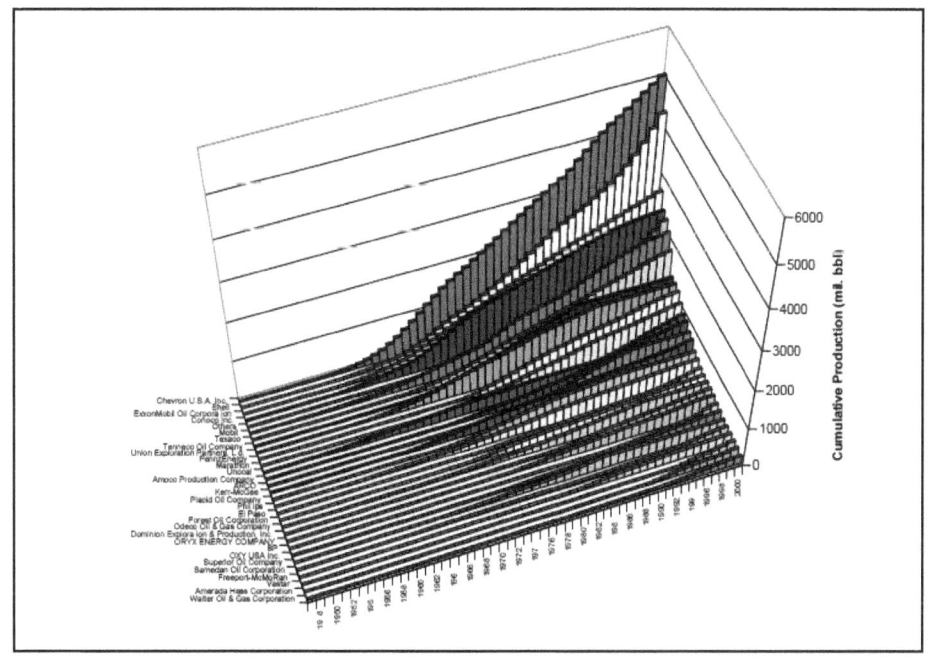

Figure 2.2: Cumulative Oil and Gas Production by Firms from the Gulf of Mexico OCS
Measured in Barrels of Oil Equivalent, 1947-2001.

The degree or extent of competition for OCS oil and gas leases can be characterized by the number and relative size of firms in the lease auction market, the number of bids or bidders per lease and other related attributes and measures. The larger the number of participants, the more competitive is the lease auction market. But since participants can bid alone (solo bids) or together (joint bids), the number of participants by itself is not an unambiguous indicator of the degree or nature of competition.

Whether joint bidding increases or decreases competition for leases is still a debatable question. Joint bidding may serve to introduce new firms and allow smaller firms to participate, thus promoting competition, or it may diminish competition by allowing firms who are potential competitors to cooperate or collude. Moreover, a principal policy MMS uses to promote competition or limit market power is to prohibit the largest firms from submitting joint bids together.

An ex post indicator of competition is the extent to which leases are concentrated. If leases are won or held predominately by a few firms, the implication is that competition has been less effective or intense than if leases were distributed more evenly or broadly. This latter way of measuring competitiveness has been used traditionally by economists to study competition and market structure, and we will begin by applying it to the market or auction for leases in the Gulf of Mexico.

**Table 2.1** presents trends in the commonly used indicators of industry structure and competitiveness, concentration ratios, the number of firms bidding for OCS leases and the Herfindahl Index (HHI).

*Number of Firms participating in Lease Sales:* The number of firms participating in lease sales varies from sale to sale as is illustrated in the second column of **Table 2.1**. The steepest contraction of competitors was in 1986 when the world oil price collapsed, creating considerable uncertainty in all energy markets. With that exception, however, the number of participants usually has been within a range of roughly 65 to 95 firms annually. The number of firms that participated in at least one sale during the entire period is much larger, about 290.

*Concentration Ratio*: A traditional measure used to study industrial organization and anti-trust trends and issues is the share of the industry owned by the largest four, eight or twenty firms. In our case there is a question of how "share" ought to be defined and measured. The most direct way is probably, simply, as the share of ownership of oil and gas leases in the OCS awarded to the top four or the top eight firms, which is shown in **Table 2.1**. To calculate the ratios, leases won at the annual bidding process on the OCS were arranged by firm in a descending order and a lease share was calculated for each firm in each sale-year.[2]

---

[2] Jointly-owned leases were allocated to firms according to their percentage share of the lease (a convention followed throughout the study).

Table 2.1

Measures of Competitiveness Based on Leases Acquired, 1983 to 1999

| Year | Number of Firms | Percent of Leases Held by | | | HHI |
|---|---|---|---|---|---|
| | | Top 4 | Top 8 | Top 20 | |
| 1983 | 92 | 28.5 | 44.8 | 71.4 | 367 |
| 1984 | 81 | 28.8 | 46.0 | 73.4 | 381 |
| 1985 | 74 | 38.9 | 53.6 | 76.1 | 552 |
| 1986 | 45 | 49.3 | 66.3 | 89.3 | 870 |
| 1987 | 68 | 45.8 | 63.9 | 84.8 | 829 |
| 1988 | 92 | 42.7 | 56.5 | 79.0 | 908 |
| 1989 | 87 | 45.4 | 57.1 | 77.6 | 865 |
| 1990 | 94 | 36.8 | 49.1 | 72.2 | 430 |
| 1991 | 83 | 28.6 | 46.7 | 70.0 | 373 |
| 1992 | 63 | 24.9 | 40.7 | 71.7 | 335 |
| 1993 | 65 | 32.1 | 49.2 | 74.9 | 425 |
| 1994 | 87 | 24.8 | 41.6 | 64.9 | 308 |
| 1995 | 86 | 30.2 | 45.6 | 70.8 | 371 |
| 1996 | 91 | 34.6 | 52.6 | 74.8 | 456 |
| 1997 | 101 | 32.6 | 49.6 | 71.5 | 453 |
| 1998 | 87 | 34.2 | 56.5 | 77.8 | 486 |
| 1999 | 72 | 30.0 | 45.9 | 74.4 | 411 |
| 1983-1990 | 176 | 33.0 | 46.8 | 68.9 | 480 |
| 1990-1999 | 207 | 25.0 | 40.9 | 64.9 | 307 |
| 1983-1999 | 290 | 26.5 | 41.7 | 63.2 | 337 |

The four-firm ratio is the sum of the market shares of the top four firms, while the eight-firm concentration ratio is the sum of market shares for the top eight firms. In 1986, the top four winners of OCS leases accounted for 49.3 percent, the highest share during the 1983 – 1999 period. By 1999, the share of the top four firms was only 30 percent, about a four percent deviation from the overall average share over the period. The share of the top eight firms also declined from a high of 66.3 percent in 1986 to a low of 40.7 in 1992, a decline that is slightly more than 25 percent.

The shares of leases won by the top four and the top eight firms seem to be quite stable over the period, with the exception of the first four or five years after the crude oil prices collapsed in 1986. The increasing shares observed from 1985 to 1988 probably reflected the exodus of smaller firms from lease sales in response to the collapse of crude oil prices.

*Herfindahl Index:* Concentration ratios by themselves do not reveal the relative sizes of the firms within the groups nor within the rest of the market. A deviation from competitive behavior and performance may occur if there are significant differences in the relative market shares. The Herfindahl index (HHI) measures both the absolute and the relative concentration of the market shares. The HHI is defined as the sum of the squares of the market shares of all participating firms in the lease auction market in a given period or year—considering the size of all participants, not just the largest four or largest eight.

Usually, the industry or market competitiveness is broadly characterized using the magnitude of the HHI index. A market that has an HHI of less than 1,000 is less concentrated and can be described as being competitive. Dougher (1987) argues that a market is moderately concentrated if its HHI lies between 1000 and 1,800, or highly concentrated when HHI is greater than 1,800.

Application of this categorization to lease sales from 1983-1999 suggests that the market for OCS oil and gas leases is not concentrated. In fact, the lease market has become less concentrated with time. **Table 2.1** shows that the HHI in 1988 was 908, the closest to 1000 level during the period. By 1999, the estimated HHI was 411, a decline of nearly 500 units. The average HHI for the 1983 to 1990 period was 480, and it fell to 307 during the 1990-1999 interval.

Leases are held for varying terms. Some are turned back after their initial 5-year term, others are held as long as there is production or other activity such as pumping. Thus the stock or inventory of active leases that a firm controls will differ from the number of leases it acquires. The concentration ratios calculated on the basis of currently active leases are: 34 percent of active leases were held by the top four firms, 48 percent by the largest eight, and 71 percent for the largest twenty firms.[3] Although these are current rather than average or cumulative measures, they are only marginally larger than the averages for the 1990 to 1999 period shown in **Table 2.1** of 25 percent, 41 percent and 65 percent, respectively. The HHI for active leases of 406 is also reasonably close to the 1990 to 1999 HHI of 307.

*Leases or Production as the Basis for Measurement*: Implicit in some analysis and regulation of the petroleum industry is the idea that the relevant indicator of potential market power is production. **Table 2.2** reports the same data as is shown in **Table 2.1**, except that the concentration ratios and HHI index are calculated with production rather than leases acquired.

Comparing the tables indicates that measures based on leases acquired are both more variable and indicate less concentration than do the same measures based on production. The average HHI value over the 1983 to 1999 period was 624 using production, contrasted to an HHI of 337 using leases acquired. Similarly the average percentage of production accounted for by the top 20 firms over the period was 84 percent as opposed to 63 percent of the leases acquired.

Using a production base yields higher concentration ratios and HHI values, but neither measure reaches levels that have traditionally been used to delineate a concentrated industry. Although the average HHI index for the production based measure almost doubles, it still falls well short of the 1000 value commonly used to divide competitive from noncompetitive markets.

---

[3] The authors calculated these figures in a separate document, using MMS data.

Table 2.2

Measures of Competitiveness Based on Production in the Gulf of Mexico OCS

| Year | # Firms | Top 4 | Top 8 | Top 20 | HHI |
|---|---|---|---|---|---|
| 1983 | 55 | 39 | 64 | 93 | 643 |
| 1984 | 58 | 38 | 63 | 92 | 629 |
| 1985 | 60 | 39 | 65 | 93 | 651 |
| 1986 | 64 | 39 | 64 | 93 | 641 |
| 1987 | 67 | 40 | 65 | 93 | 662 |
| 1988 | 70 | 39 | 64 | 93 | 650 |
| 1989 | 76 | 39 | 62 | 91 | 623 |
| 1990 | 87 | 43 | 66 | 91 | 688 |
| 1991 | 94 | 45 | 68 | 90 | 730 |
| 1992 | 97 | 45 | 69 | 90 | 747 |
| 1993 | 101 | 45 | 70 | 89 | 760 |
| 1994 | 104 | 43 | 66 | 87 | 708 |
| 1995 | 109 | 42 | 64 | 86 | 672 |
| 1996 | 109 | 45 | 63 | 84 | 701 |
| 1997 | 111 | 44 | 61 | 82 | 668 |
| 1998 | 111 | 43 | 60 | 80 | 650 |
| 1999 | 105 | 43 | 61 | 83 | 674 |
| 1983-1990 | 100 | 39 | 64 | 92 | 637 |
| 1990-1999 | 196 | 44 | 63 | 83 | 671 |
| 1983-1999 | 222 | 42 | 61 | 84 | 624 |

If production is used to make the calculations, there is also a question of whether production in the Gulf of Mexico (GOM), U.S. or domestic production or global production is the appropriate measure to use. Some regulation, including MMS' own Restricted Joint Bidders List, uses global production as an indicator of potential market power.

**Table 2.3** shows the GOM production, GOM leases, U.S. production, and global production for each of the companies that ranked in the top 50 in either GOM production or leases on a cumulative basis during the 1990s.

The firm-by-firm summary shown in **Table 2.3** underscores the wide variation in type of firm and extent of participation in the GOM lease market. Shell, the largest GOM producer during the period was also the largest global producer, but ranked behind ARCO and Exxon and only slightly ahead of Chevron and Texaco in U.S. production. At the other end of the distribution were small companies like King Ranch operating only in the GOM but also large international companies like Petrobras with small GOM production but larger global production than some U.S. majors.

Table 2.3

Gulf of Mexico (GOM) Production and Leases, U.S. Production and Global Production for the
Top 50 Firms in Either GOM Production or Leases, 1990 to 1999

| Company | Totals: 1990-1999 | | | |
|---|---|---|---|---|
| | U.S. GOM MMBOE | U.S. GOM, Leases Acquired | WORLD MMBOE | U.S. MMBOE |
| Agip | 71 | 55 | 3,365 | 71 |
| Amerada | 205 | 207 | 1,287 | 498 |
| Amoco | 341 | 243 | 3,916 | 1,972 |
| Anadarko | 50 | 71 | 397 | 384 |
| Apache | 124 | 45 | 439 | 382 |
| ARCO | 182 | 109 | 3,546 | 2,867 |
| Basin | 11 | 33 | 24 | 24 |
| BHP | 20 | 207 | 100 | 81 |
| BP | 315 | 418 | 6,449 | 1,953 |
| British-Borneo | 20 | 64 | 32 | 20 |
| Burlington | 47 | 79 | 525 | 459 |
| Chevron | 1,449 | 494 | 5,150 | 2,669 |
| Chieftain | 2 | 57 | 44 | 41 |
| CNG | 187 | 77 | 77 | 77 |
| Coastal | 69 | 72 | 295 | 295 |
| Conoco | 382 | 268 | 2,101 | 862 |
| Cxy | 29 | 62 | 541 | 43 |
| Elf | 55 | 62 | 3,599 | 55 |
| Energy Development | 44 | 30 | 106 | 100 |
| Enron | 94 | 115 | 403 | 354 |
| Enserch | 33 | 60 | 174 | 175 |
| Exxon | 595 | 354 | 8,415 | 3,126 |
| Fina | . | 41 | 114 | 114 |
| Forcenergy | 54 | 26 | 52 | 52 |
| Forest | 121 | 27 | 90 | 71 |
| Freeport | 84 | 10 | 51 | 51 |
| Hall-Houston | 84 | 28 | 84 | 84 |
| Houston Exploration | 37 | 63 | 13 | 13 |
| Kerr-McGee | 199 | 161 | 515 | 305 |
| King Ranch | 8 | 34 | 8 | 8 |
| Louisiana L&E | 63 | 82 | 218 | 150 |
| Marathon | 328 | 110 | 1,284 | 328 |
| Mobil | 629 | 341 | 5,248 | 1,758 |
| Murphy | 146 | 115 | 332 | 151 |
| Nerco | 55 | 15 | 55 | 55 |
| Newfield | 160 | 33 | 75 | 74 |
| Nippon | 5 | 38 | 5 | 5 |
| Norcen | 96 | 45 | 2 | 24 |
| Ocean Energy | 35 | 24 | 131 | 99 |

Table 2.3: Gulf of Mexico (GOM) Production and Leases, U.S. Production and Global Production for the Top 50 Firms in Either GOM Production or Leases, 1990 to 1999 (continued)

| | Totals: 1990-1999 | | | |
|---|---|---|---|---|
| Company | U.S. GOM MMBOE | U.S. GOM, Leases Acquired | WORLD MMBOE | U.S. MMBOE |
| Oxy | 162 | 18 | 1,374 | 624 |
| Pennzoil | 372 | 96 | 478 | 460 |
| Petrobras | 4 | 35 | 3,311 | 4 |
| Petsec | 24 | 35 | 9 | 9 |
| Phillips | 113 | 89 | 1,838 | 1,017 |
| Pogo | 44 | 31 | 127 | 117 |
| Samedan | 187 | 104 | 301 | 275 |
| Santa Fe | 62 | 65 | 346 | 308 |
| Seagull | 59 | 89 | 171 | 138 |
| Seneca | 41 | 42 | 19 | 19 |
| Shell | 1,579 | 789 | 12,504 | 2,703 |
| Sonat | 101 | 64 | 302 | 302 |
| Statoil | 4 | 35 | 7 | 7 |
| Sun | . | 138 | 481 | . |
| Texaco | 547 | 404 | 4,235 | 2,640 |
| Umc | 16 | 36 | 57 | 41 |
| Union Pacific | 87 | 68 | 912 | 819 |
| Unocal | 511 | 288 | 1,935 | 1,058 |
| Vastar | 212 | 242 | 212 | 212 |
| Walter | 159 | 52 | 159 | 159 |
| Zilkha | 62 | 348 | 62 | 62 |

As illustrated in **Figure 2.3**, the "GOM-top-50" accounted for slightly more than 90 percent of GOM production over the 1990 through 1999 interval, and almost 55 percent of total U.S. production. However, they only accounted for 22.4 percent of global production during the same period.

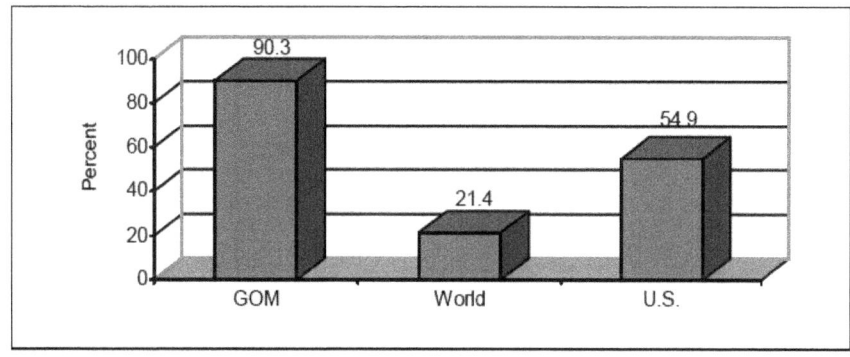

Figure 2.3: Share of Production from the U.S. GOM, U.S. and the World for the Top 50 Firms Operating in the U.S. Gulf of Mexico OCS

**Table 2.4** compares the top four, top eight and top twenty concentration ratios and HHI indexes based on GOM production and U.S. production on an annual basis for the 1990s. As might be expected, the ratios and index based on the total U.S. petroleum production are somewhat below the ratios and index calculated with GOM production, but the differences are not large.

**Table 2.5** combines the two bases of measurement for the GOM (leases acquired and production) by showing concentration ratios measured as the share of leases acquired by the top four, top eight and top twenty firms, but using their production over the preceding 10 year period to define who the top four, etc., were.

Comparing **Tables 2.1** and **2.2** indicates both less year-to-year variation and more concentration if production, rather than leases acquired, is used as the basis of the measurement. When the two approaches are combined as in **Table 2.5** with leases acquired by the top four, eight, or twenty firms ranked in terms of production during the preceding ten years, measures of concentration fall and year-to-year variation in measurements increases markedly. This is not unexpected since firms, especially larger firms who have been active in the Gulf in the previous ten years, accumulate inventories of leases that can be either increased or drawn down if circumstances change.

**Table 2.6** lists the number of leases acquired and total barrels of oil equivalent produced in the Gulf of Mexico OCS during the 1990 to 1999 period for the top twenty firms in both categories. Shell and Chevron are one and two in both categories, and the first fifteen or so ranks correspond fairly closely. However, there are also some significant differences. BP is ranked eleventh in production but third in leases won. Zilkha obtained 348 leases during the period which was the sixth highest, but it was only 37th in production.[4] At the other extreme, Newfield was 19th in production but only 39th in leases acquired.

Differences among firms resulting from timing and strategy are evident in both rankings. The leasing of most of the deep tracts in the Gulf occurred in the 1995-1997 lease sales. In 1995 there were 1012 active leases in water deeper than 800 meters. By 1998 this number had almost tripled to 3002.[5] Some firms acquired leases very aggressively and successfully but production will lag leasing by at least five or six years. Conversely, other firms such as Newfield have followed a strategy of acquiring properties by means other than lease sales.

The last two columns in **Table 2.6** indicate the number of times the firms listed were among the top 20 firms in the production or leasing categories from 1990-1999. The irregular nature of the industry over the short or intermediate term is indicated by fact that three of the firms ranked as top ten producers over the period were ranked as top 20 producers in only five or fewer years.

---

[4] Zilkha Energy Company's history illustrates one of the difficulties in analyzing the lease market's performance—the frequency of changes in ownership and control. A very active participant in the 1990s, Zilkha was purchased by Sonat, another large independent, for $1Billion in stock in January of 1998. Sonat was then purchased by El Paso Energy Corp. for $6 Billion in October of 1999.

[5] Baud, R.D. et al. Deepwater Gulf of Mexico 2002, p.14.

Table 2.4

Concentration Ratios (shown as percentages),
HHI Indices and Total Production for the U.S. & the Gulf of Mexico OCS

| Year | OCS | | | | U.S. | | | |
|------|-------|-------|--------|-----|-------|-------|--------|-----|
|      | Top 4 | Top 8 | Top 20 | HHI | Top 4 | Top 8 | Top 20 | HHI |
| 1990 | 43 | 66 | 91 | 688 | 34 | 61 | 82 | 521 |
| 1991 | 45 | 68 | 90 | 730 | 34 | 60 | 82 | 516 |
| 1992 | 45 | 69 | 90 | 747 | 33 | 59 | 82 | 499 |
| 1993 | 45 | 70 | 89 | 760 | 31 | 56 | 79 | 461 |
| 1994 | 43 | 66 | 87 | 708 | 31 | 56 | 79 | 454 |
| 1995 | 42 | 64 | 86 | 672 | 31 | 55 | 78 | 446 |
| 1996 | 45 | 63 | 84 | 701 | 30 | 53 | 76 | 429 |
| 1997 | 44 | 61 | 82 | 668 | 30 | 53 | 76 | 425 |
| 1998 | 43 | 60 | 81 | 650 | 35 | 55 | 76 | 472 |
| 1999 | 43 | 61 | 83 | 674 | 38 | 56 | 77 | 522 |

Table 2.5

Share of Leases Acquired by Top 4, 8, and 20 Producing Firms[a]

| Year | No. Firms | Top 4 | Top 8 | Top 20 | HHI |
|------|-----------|-------|-------|--------|-----|
| 1983 | 55 | 20 | 31 | 57 | 643 |
| 1984 | 58 | 20 | 29 | 51 | 629 |
| 1985 | 60 | 30 | 40 | 60 | 651 |
| 1986 | 64 | 45 | 50 | 75 | 641 |
| 1987 | 67 | 36 | 52 | 78 | 662 |
| 1988 | 70 | 36 | 46 | 67 | 650 |
| 1989 | 76 | 35 | 41 | 54 | 623 |
| 1990 | 87 | 19 | 26 | 47 | 688 |
| 1991 | 94 | 27 | 40 | 49 | 730 |
| 1992 | 97 | 17 | 24 | 31 | 747 |
| 1993 | 101 | 11 | 19 | 27 | 760 |
| 1994 | 104 | 16 | 20 | 28 | 708 |
| 1995 | 109 | 27 | 34 | 45 | 672 |
| 1996 | 109 | 24 | 37 | 46 | 701 |
| 1997 | 111 | 28 | 39 | 56 | 668 |
| 1998 | 111 | 30 | 54 | 66 | 650 |
| 1999 | 105 | 5 | 13 | 49 | 674 |
| 1983-1999 | 222 | 25 | 37 | 53 | 637 |
| 1983-1990 | 100 | 28 | 39 | 60 | 671 |
| 1990-1999 | 196 | 24 | 35 | 49 | 624 |

[a] Ranking is based on immediate past ten years' production.

29

Table 2.6

Top 20 Firms in Total Oil and Gas Production or
Total Leases Acquired in the Gulf of Mexico, 1990-1999

| Company | Rank | | Production | Leases | FT20 | |
|---|---|---|---|---|---|---|
| | Production | Leases | MMBOE | Number | Production | Leases |
| Shell | 1 | 1 | 1,579 | 789 | 10 | 10 |
| Chevron | 2 | 2 | 1,449 | 494 | 8 | 8 |
| Mobil | 3 | 7 | 629 | 341 | 9 | 9 |
| Exxon | 4 | 5 | 595 | 354 | 7 | 7 |
| Texaco | 5 | 4 | 547 | 404 | 9 | 9 |
| Unocal | 6 | 8 | 511 | 288 | 5 | 5 |
| Conoco | 7 | 9 | 382 | 268 | 6 | 6 |
| Pennzoil | 8 | 21 | 372 | 96 | 4 | 0 |
| Amoco | 9 | 10 | 341 | 243 | 7 | 7 |
| Marathon | 10 | 18 | 328 | 110 | 4 | 4 |
| BP | 11 | 3 | 315 | 418 | 7 | 7 |
| Vastar | 12 | 11 | 212 | 242 | 6 | 6 |
| Amerada | 13 | 13 | 205 | 207 | 9 | 9 |
| Kerr-McGee | 14 | 14 | 199 | 161 | 7 | 7 |
| Samedan | 15 | 20 | 187 | 104 | 5 | 5 |
| CNG | 16 | 26 | 187 | 77 | 4 | 0 |
| ARCO | 17 | 19 | 182 | 109 | 4 | 4 |
| Oxy | 18 | 71 | 162 | 18 | 0 | 0 |
| Newfield | 19 | 53 | 160 | 33 | 0 | 0 |
| Walter | 20 | 39 | 159 | 52 | 0 | 0 |
| Murphy | 21 | 16 | 146 | 115 | 0 | 5 |
| Enron | 28 | 17 | 94 | 115 | 0 | 6 |
| Zilkha | 37 | 6 | 62 | 348 | 0 | 6 |
| BHP | 68 | 12 | 20 | 207 | 0 | 7 |
| Sun | - | 15 | 0 | 138 | 0 | 7 |

*Number of Bids per Lease:* **Table 2.7** presents two attributes commonly used to describe the degree of competition in lease auction markets, the number of bids per lease and number of bidders per lease.

Table 2.7

Measures of the Intensity of Competition for OCS Leases

| Year | All Bids | | Competitive Bids (More than One Bid) | |
|---|---|---|---|---|
| | Bids/Lease | Bidders/Lease | Bids/Lease | Bidders/Lease |
| 1983 | 1.64 | 3.51 | 2.86 | 6.31 |
| 1984 | 1.49 | 3.01 | 2.59 | 5.58 |
| 1985 | 1.39 | 2.58 | 2.56 | 4.98 |
| 1986 | 1.17 | 1.68 | 2.13 | 2.74 |
| 1987 | 1.33 | 1.68 | 2.49 | 3.17 |
| 1988 | 1.36 | 1.79 | 2.67 | 3.76 |
| 1989 | 1.39 | 1.82 | 2.66 | 3.84 |
| 1990 | 1.55 | 2.02 | 2.76 | 3.83 |
| 1991 | 1.35 | 1.85 | 2.49 | 3.62 |
| 1992 | 1.31 | 1.91 | 2.33 | 3.67 |
| 1993 | 1.28 | 1.58 | 2.52 | 3.52 |
| 1994 | 1.48 | 2.09 | 2.63 | 3.89 |
| 1995 | 1.42 | 1.98 | 2.61 | 3.78 |
| 1996 | 1.50 | 2.07 | 2.71 | 3.83 |
| 1997 | 1.64 | 2.26 | 2.85 | 4.03 |
| 1998 | 1.40 | 1.88 | 2.89 | 4.17 |
| 1999 | 1.25 | 1.62 | 2.51 | 3.46 |
| 1983-1989 | 1.44 | 2.41 | 2.66 | 4.85 |
| 1990-1999 | 1.48 | 2.01 | 2.73 | 3.89 |
| 1983-1999 | 1.46 | 2.17 | 2.70 | 4.26 |

On average there were more bids per lease in the 1990s than in the 1980s. But there also were fewer participants in the bidding process on a per lease basis. This is true whether the bids were competitive or noncompetitive. The average number of bids per lease increased from 1.44 for the period 1983-1989 to 1.48 for the period 1990-1999. However, the mean value for the number of bidders decreased from 2.41 to 2.01 during the same periods. For leases with at least two bids per lease, i.e., competitive bids, the overall average number of bids per lease for the period 1983-1999, was 2.70. This measure also increased from the 1983-1989 average of 2.66 to an average of 2.73 between 1990 and 1999.

A pictorial view of the overall trend in bids per lease, which incorporates estimated values from previous studies, is presented in **Figure 2.4**. The number of bids per lease was 2.72 for 1954-1966 and 3.90 for 1966-1977 (Mead and Sorensen, 1980). Erickson and Spann (1974) also estimated the average number of bids per tract over the period 1954-1973 for the entire U.S. OCS as 3.56 and Saidi and Marsden (1992) estimated bids per lease for the period 1973-1977 as 2.96. These estimates were made prior to 1983 when area-wide leasing policy began on the OCS.

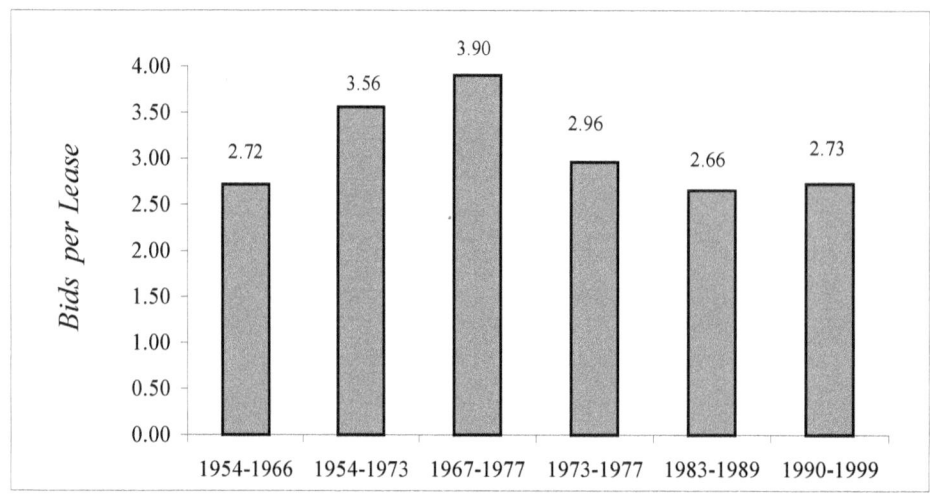

Figure 2.4: Average Number of Bids Per Lease in Different Periods.

Competition measured in terms of bids per lease on the OCS, on average, appears to be significantly less intense during the period 1983-1999 compared to earlier history. The reason for the overall decline in bids per lease is evident in the frequency distribution of bids per lease presented in **Table 2.8.** On average, the proportion of leases with just one bid from 1983 to 1999 was 75 percent. The proportion of leases receiving at least three bids was less than 10 percent during this period. Erickson and Spann (1974)[6] reported that nearly 70 percent of leases had three or more bids during the period 1969-1973.

### 2.3 Bidding Arrangements for OCS Leases

Firms seeking the right to explore and develop petroleum resources on the Gulf OCS participate in lease sales either by bidding alone in solo ventures or by bidding as a partner with other firms through joint ventures. By definition, joint ventures reduce the number of potential bidders. Thus they might be considered to tend to reduce competition in the lease market. But, joint venturing may also increase the number of actual bidders by facilitating the entry of relatively smaller operators into offshore E&P ventures, ventures that are by most standards risky and capital intensive. Joint ventures allow for the pooling of resources together to meet the minimum capital requirement for acquiring petroleum leases. Thus, it has been suggested that the incidence of joint ventures and the number of bidders or bids should be positively correlated (Erickson and Spann, 1974; Saidi and Marsden, 1992; and Markham, 1970).

Of the 20, 361 bids submitted from 1983-1999 for the right to explore and develop 14,300 leases in the Gulf of Mexico OCS, joint ventures accounted for 32 percent. Nearly 50 percent of the 20,361 bids were for leases that attracted at least two bids (competitive). Joint ventures were involved in 38.4 percent of bids submitted for competitive leases. In contrast, less than 28 percent of the single-bid leases (non competitive) were made jointly.

---

[6] See Erickson and Spann (1974) Table 2, Page 1701.

Table 2.8

Percentage Frequency Distribution of Leases by the Number of Bids

| | Number of Bids/Lease | | | | | | |
|---|---|---|---|---|---|---|---|
| Year | 1 | 2 | 3 | 4 | 5 | 6 | >6 |
| 1983 | 65.8 | 19.8 | 6.9 | 3.6 | 2.1 | 0.9 | 1.0 |
| 1984 | 69.2 | 20.7 | 5.3 | 2.8 | 1.4 | 0.2 | 0.4 |
| 1985 | 75.1 | 17.7 | 3.2 | 2.3 | 1.2 | 0.2 | 0.3 |
| 1986 | 85.2 | 12.9 | 1.9 | 0.0 | 0.0 | 0.0 | 0.0 |
| 1987 | 77.9 | 15.3 | 4.3 | 1.9 | 0.0 | 0.4 | 0.1 |
| 1988 | 78.2 | 14.8 | 3.1 | 2.5 | 0.6 | 0.3 | 0.4 |
| 1989 | 76.6 | 15.7 | 4.7 | 1.6 | 0.3 | 0.4 | 0.7 |
| 1990 | 69.1 | 18.5 | 6.6 | 3.6 | 0.9 | 0.4 | 0.9 |
| 1991 | 76.4 | 16.0 | 5.0 | 1.8 | 0.7 | 0.0 | 0.2 |
| 1992 | 76.9 | 17.0 | 4.7 | 1.4 | 0.0 | 0.0 | 0.0 |
| 1993 | 81.6 | 13.1 | 2.2 | 2.2 | 0.6 | 0.3 | 0.0 |
| 1994 | 70.8 | 19.1 | 5.1 | 3.2 | 1.0 | 0.2 | 0.5 |
| 1995 | 73.7 | 17.5 | 5.3 | 1.6 | 0.9 | 0.5 | 0.5 |
| 1996 | 70.9 | 17.0 | 7.8 | 2.0 | 1.3 | 0.6 | 0.4 |
| 1997 | 65.4 | 18.8 | 8.8 | 3.8 | 1.5 | 0.7 | 1.0 |
| 1998 | 78.8 | 13.4 | 3.4 | 1.8 | 1.3 | 0.3 | 0.9 |
| 1999 | 83.6 | 11.7 | 2.2 | 1.4 | 1.1 | 0.0 | 0.0 |
| 1983-89 | 75.4 | 16.7 | 4.2 | 2.1 | 0.8 | 0.3 | 0.4 |
| 1990-99 | 74.7 | 16.2 | 5.1 | 2.3 | 0.9 | 0.3 | 0.4 |
| 1983-99 | 75.0 | 16.4 | 4.7 | 2.2 | 0.9 | 0.3 | 0.4 |

The decline in the share of bids submitted as joint ventures for both the competitive and noncompetitive leases may be linked to the restriction imposed on some major oil companies from being co-bidders in any joint bids[7] This restriction will be discussed in a subsequent section of this chapter. However, as the proportion of bids by joint ventures declined through time, the proportion of high bonus bids awarded to joint venture bidders also declined. In 1983, for example, about 64 percent of leases awarded in the OCS were to joint bidders compared to the less than 30 percent, on average, within the last three years (**Table 2.9**). This is comparable to the trend in the proportion of all bids submitted as joint ventures over the same period. During the first three years of lease sales after area-wide leasing began, roughly 56 percent of all bids submitted on the OCS were accounted for by joint ventures. In contrast, the proportion of bids accounted for through joint bidding from 1997-1999 was less than 30 percent on average. Overall, Erickson and Spann (1974) reported that joint ventures as a fraction of total bids increased significantly over time during the period from 1954–1977.

---

[7] The Energy Policy Conservation Act, enacted in 1976, banned companies from submitting bids jointly in federal OCS lease sales, if their global petroleum production is in excess of 1.6 millions barrels of oil equivalent per day (Moody and Kruvant, 1988; Sullivan et al., 1980) The list of restricted joint bidders is published in the U.S. Federal Register.

Table 2.9

Percent Share of Bids that were Joint Venture Bids

| Year | Single Bids | | At Least Two Bids | |
|---|---|---|---|---|
| | All Bids | High Bids | All Bids | High Bids |
| 1983 | 63.9 | 62.0 | 66.0 | 64.4 |
| 1984 | 53.5 | 49.3 | 60.9 | 59.2 |
| 1985 | 46.1 | 45.6 | 49.3 | 52.1 |
| 1986 | 30.4 | 29.7 | 26.5 | 17.4 |
| 1987 | 18.8 | 19.6 | 21.4 | 28.7 |
| 1988 | 23.9 | 22.0 | 29.7 | 30.8 |
| 1989 | 22.8 | 19.0 | 32.1 | 31.3 |
| 1990 | 22.5 | 20.6 | 27.6 | 30.7 |
| 1991 | 28.2 | 27.4 | 32.9 | 36.4 |
| 1992 | 33.6 | 31.1 | 41.2 | 40.8 |
| 1993 | 19.2 | 18.4 | 28.9 | 39.4 |
| 1994 | 31.2 | 28.9 | 36.3 | 36.8 |
| 1995 | 27.8 | 26.0 | 31.6 | 30.8 |
| 1996 | 28.5 | 30.0 | 30.3 | 38.8 |
| 1997 | 29.1 | 29.6 | 30.7 | 35.1 |
| 1998 | 27.7 | 25.5 | 33.8 | 35.2 |
| 1999 | 23.6 | 22.8 | 31.8 | 39.0 |
| 1983-89 | 37.1 | 35.3 | 40.8 | 40.6 |
| 1990-99 | 27.1 | 26.0 | 32.5 | 36.3 |
| 1983-99 | 31.2 | 29.9 | 35.9 | 38.1 |

## 2.4 Characterizing the Market for OCS Leases

*The Value of High Bonus Bid:* The value of high bonus bids provides a measure of the initial cash payment to the government for granting firms the right to explore in the OCS region per lease awarded. As such it is an important variable to monitor and understand. It is not, of course, the only or necessarily the most important indicator of the performance of the lease market. The fundamental goal of the leasing program is to facilitate the efficient exploration and development of the nation's petroleum resources. High bonus bids may be either "too high" or "too low" to accomplish this goal (McDonald, 1979).

This is true even if the policy perspective is limited to government revenues rather than national economic output or efficiency. Over the 1982 to 2000 period the federal treasury received about $57 billion in offshore royalties and rental payments and about $24 billion in bonus payments from lease sales.[8] More recently this difference has grown.

---

[8] These totals include payments for non-oil and gas minerals; they are not significant enough to bias the comparison.

In the year 2000, for example, offshore oil and gas royalties, plus rental payments on active leases on which production has not yet begun, amounted to about $4.3 billion which is almost ten times as much as the $442 million in total bonus bid payments which were received from lease sales in that year. Thus, if bidding at lease sales were so intense that exploration and development were discouraged it is possible that royalties would fall enough to reduce total OCS revenues going to the Treasury.

- The total value of bonus bids paid during the 1983 to 1999 period was $16.720 billion and the mean value of high bonus bids per lease was about $1.12 million.

- When leases were won through competitive joint venture bidding, the average value of the high bonus bid per lease was $3.29 million, more than twice the value for noncompetitive, joint venture, high bonus bids, which was $1.18 million.

- The average high bonus bid for competitive solo venture bids for the period 1983-1999 was $1.75 million in comparison to an average high bid value of $0.614 million for noncompetitive solo ventures.[9]

Thus, consistently, the data show higher bonus bids for competitive leases than for noncompetitive leases, irrespective of the type of bid (**Tables 2.10** and **2.11**). It is important to note that a joint venture bid on a lease is counted as one bid irrespective of the number of participating partners in the winning joint venture.

The relationship between the average value of high bonus bids and number of bids is illustrated in **Figure 2.5**. The value of the high bonus bids, on average, tends to increase with the number of bids per lease.

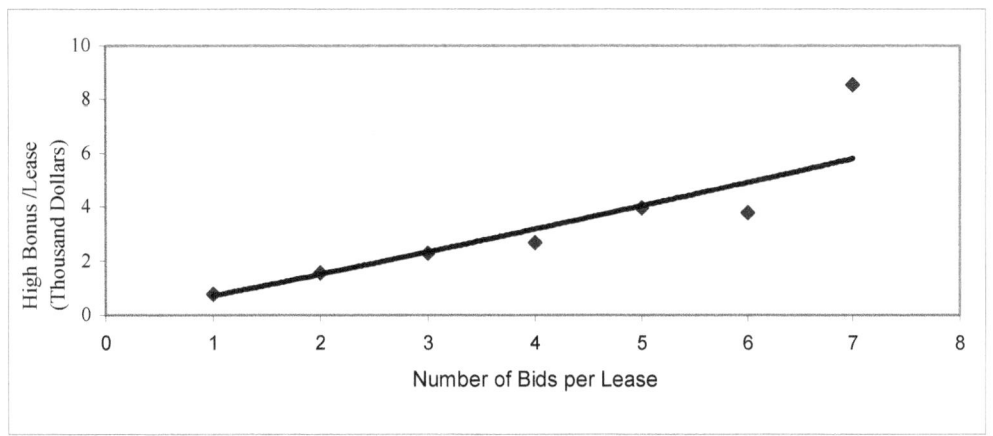

Figure 2.5: Trend in the Value of the High Bonus Bids, 1983-1999.

---

[9] The authors calculated these figures in a separate document, using MMS data.

Table 2.10

Average Value of High Bonus Bids,
1983 to 1999 (in thousands of dollars)

| YEAR | Noncompetitive Bids | | | Competitive Bids | | |
|------|------|-------|------|------|-------|------|
| | Solo | Joint | All | Solo | Joint | All |
| 1983 | 3,023 | 2,608 | 2,771 | 6,357 | 9,060 | 8,099 |
| 1984 | 1,717 | 1,998 | 1,843 | 4,043 | 4,308 | 4,200 |
| 1985 | 1,558 | 1,858 | 1,688 | 3,595 | 5,051 | 4,354 |
| 1986 | 1,182 | 1,258 | 1,206 | 1,844 | 2,234 | 1,912 |
| 1987 | 572 | 864 | 621 | 1,153 | 1,876 | 1,360 |
| 1988 | 376 | 417 | 384 | 1,145 | 1,303 | 1,194 |
| 1989 | 383 | 731 | 436 | 1,111 | 1,375 | 1,194 |
| 1990 | 449 | 455 | 450 | 1,282 | 1,190 | 1,254 |
| 1991 | 363 | 486 | 393 | 1,040 | 881 | 982 |
| 1992 | 283 | 323 | 294 | 726 | 888 | 792 |
| 1993 | 262 | 429 | 285 | 635 | 950 | 759 |
| 1994 | 270 | 507 | 331 | 1,202 | 1,120 | 1,172 |
| 1995 | 288 | 323 | 296 | 1,051 | 972 | 1,027 |
| 1996 | 321 | 478 | 363 | 1,035 | 1,129 | 1,071 |
| 1997 | 397 | 692 | 476 | 1,228 | 1,623 | 1,366 |
| 1998 | 547 | 1,046 | 662 | 2,053 | 4,531 | 2,925 |
| 1999 | 482 | 1,010 | 586 | 1,216 | 2,013 | 1,527 |

A pictorial view of the trend in the index of mean value of high bonus bids for the period is presented in **Figure 2.6**. The index is defined as the value of high bonus bids per lease in each year divided by the mean value from 1983-1999.

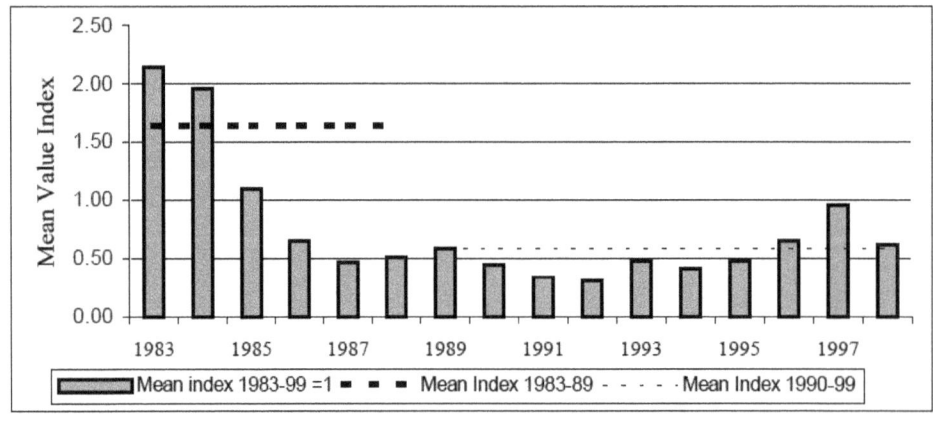

Figure 2.6: Trend in the Index of the Annual Average Value of High Bids.

Table 2.11 lists the top 20 firms, in either production or leases acquired, and their average high bids for leases over the 1990 to 1999 time period. Average high bids are shown for all leases (total in column 4) shallow leases (less than 800 meters water depth), deepwater leases (more than 800 meters), competitive leases (two or more bids submitted) and noncompetitive leases (acquired with a solo bid). The variation observed among firms seems large, especially at the extremes of the distributions. For all bids, the average ranges from Marathon's high of $1,418,000 to a low of $186,000 for Zilkha—a ratio of 7.6. Further, neither of these firms were small or marginal participants in the lease market. Marathon ranked 10th in production and 18th in leases acquired while Zilkha was the sixth highest in terms of leases and 37th in production. It might be expected that the variation among leases would narrow if leases were subdivided into shallow/deep and competitive/noncompetitive categories, but the high/low ratios actually increase.

A more comprehensive measure of the relative variation of the distributions can be made by expressing the standard deviation of the series as a proportion, or percentage, of the mean of the distribution. By this measurement only the competitive series is less varied than the total series. The standard deviation as a percent of the mean is:

- 46 percent for the all bids considered as a single series,
- 54 percent for the shallow bids,
- 86 percent for deep water bids,
- 51 percent for noncompetitive bids, and
- 41 percent for competitive bids.[10]

In addition to the categorization of leases listed in the columns of Table 2.11, corporate strategy, development strategy, experience, development objectives, and a host of other factors are related to the differences in average high bids among the firms listed in the table. Identifying and incorporating such factors into our analysis in a comprehensive way exceeds the scope of this project. However, we try to facilitate the comparison of patterns in bidding results among firms by showing the normalized standard deviation or "Z-score" for each of the average high bid series in Table 2.12. The order in which firms are listed in Table 2.12 was by the firm's Z-score for all high bids (column 6). Figures 2.7-2.11 illustrate the ranking for each of the five categories in the table.

The Z-score was calculated for the top 50 firms in *either* leases or production, resulting in a sample of 63 firms. A Z-score of zero means the average high bid for the firm lies on the average of all the firms in the distribution, a Z-score of + 1.00 means the firm's average was one standard deviation above the mean of the distribution, a –1.87 means the firm's average was 1.87 standard deviations below the mean of the distribution.

---

[10] The means and standard deviations used were calculated for the "top fifty" sample shown in table 2.12, using both leases and production top 50s rankings gives a combined sample of 63 firms.

Table 2.11

Top 20 Firms in Total Oil and Gas Production or
Total Leases Acquired, Average High Bid/Lease for Total, Shallow, Deep,
Competitive and Noncompetitive Leases, 1990-1999

| Company | Production | Leases | Average High Bid (in thousands of dollars) | | | | |
|---|---|---|---|---|---|---|---|
| | MMBOE | Number | Total | Shallow | Deep | At Least Two Bids | Single Bids |
| Shell | 1,579 | 789 | 512 | 557 | 568 | 1,162 | 404 |
| Chevron | 1,449 | 494 | 364 | 337 | 480 | 1,285 | 274 |
| Mobil | 629 | 341 | 367 | 247 | 495 | 896 | 320 |
| Exxon | 595 | 354 | 487 | 657 | 478 | 1,045 | 373 |
| Texaco | 547 | 404 | 446 | 535 | 657 | 1,257 | 429 |
| Unocal | 511 | 288 | 886 | 406 | 1,386 | 2,408 | 615 |
| Conoco | 382 | 268 | 440 | 297 | 611 | 948 | 420 |
| Pennzoil | 372 | 96 | 323 | 366 | 475 | 682 | 293 |
| Amoco | 341 | 243 | 382 | 544 | 466 | 1,013 | 321 |
| Marathon | 328 | 110 | 1,418 | 1,078 | 2,354 | 2,295 | 1,635 |
| BP | 315 | 418 | 548 | 656 | 579 | 1,210 | 439 |
| Vastar | 212 | 242 | 845 | 707 | 1,432 | 1,926 | 461 |
| Amerada | 205 | 207 | 725 | 944 | 1,066 | 1,685 | 608 |
| Kerr-McGee | 199 | 161 | 1,009 | 1,508 | 1,193 | 1,894 | 1,105 |
| Samedan | 187 | 104 | 469 | 638 | 1,050 | 1,663 | 494 |
| CNG | 187 | 77 | 757 | 829 | 1,520 | 1,691 | 513 |
| ARCO | 182 | 109 | 556 | 630 | - | 1,254 | 360 |
| Oxy | 162 | 18 | 1,281 | 175 | 1,713 | 2,183 | 571 |
| Newfield | 160 | 33 | 359 | 376 | - | 571 | 289 |
| Walter | 159 | 52 | 441 | 482 | 519 | 859 | 357 |
| Murphy | 146 | 115 | 888 | 922 | 881 | 1,407 | 624 |
| Enron | 94 | 115 | 651 | 614 | 940 | 1,090 | 489 |
| Zilkha | 62 | 348 | 186 | 186 | 213 | 301 | 174 |
| BHP | 20 | 207 | 513 | 664 | 457 | 1,006 | 328 |
| Sun | 0 | 138 | 1,064 | 578 | 1,557 | 1,680 | 751 |

Table 2.12

Top 50 Firms in Either Production or Leases Acquired from 1990 to 1999 Ranked by
Z-Scores for Average High Bids, with Z-Scores for Total, Shallow, Deep,
Competitive, and Noncompetitive Average High Bids

| | Production | Leases | Rank | | Z-Score for Average High Bid | | | | |
|---|---|---|---|---|---|---|---|---|---|
| Company | MMBOE | Number | BOE | Leases | Total | Shallow | Deep | Competitive | Non-Competitive |
| Marathon | 328 | 110 | 10 | 18 | 3.20 | 1.15 | 1.32 | 1.79 | 4.29 |
| Anadarko | 50 | 71 | 42 | 28 | 2.96 | 5.55 | -0.60 | 4.14 | 0.66 |
| Statoil | 4 | 35 | 122 | 47 | 2.84 | | 0.79 | 1.44 | 4.08 |
| Elf | 55 | 62 | 40 | 34 | 1.94 | 0.14 | 0.75 | 1.66 | 1.77 |
| Oxy | 162 | 18 | 18 | 71 | 1.91 | -1.37 | 0.65 | 1.58 | 0.22 |
| Kerr-McGee | 199 | 161 | 14 | 14 | 1.52 | 2.35 | 0.10 | 1.05 | 2.27 |
| Basin | 11 | 33 | 90 | 50 | 1.15 | 1.55 | | 0.35 | 0.53 |
| British-Borneo | 20 | 64 | 67 | 32 | 0.91 | 0.82 | 0.18 | 1.10 | 0.49 |
| Sun | | 138 | | 15 | 0.73 | -0.24 | 0.48 | 0.66 | 0.91 |
| Unocal | 511 | 288 | 6 | 8 | 0.63 | -0.73 | 0.30 | 2.00 | 0.39 |
| Vastar | 212 | 242 | 12 | 11 | 0.62 | 0.12 | 0.35 | 1.11 | -0.19 |
| CNG | 187 | 77 | 16 | 26 | 0.57 | 0.46 | 0.44 | 0.68 | 0.00 |
| Burlington | 47 | 79 | 43 | 25 | 0.56 | -0.02 | 0.05 | 0.88 | 0.45 |
| Amerada | 205 | 207 | 13 | 13 | 0.50 | 0.78 | -0.04 | 0.67 | 0.37 |
| Agip | 71 | 55 | 33 | 38 | 0.44 | 0.60 | -0.05 | 1.02 | -0.17 |
| Freeport | 84 | 10 | 31 | 93 | 0.39 | 0.76 | | -0.38 | 0.06 |
| Ocean Energy | 35 | 24 | 49 | 65 | 0.38 | -0.57 | 0.33 | 0.44 | 0.24 |
| Murphy | 146 | 115 | 21 | 16 | 0.25 | 0.72 | -0.23 | 0.16 | 0.43 |
| Petsec | 24 | 35 | 64 | 48 | 0.22 | 0.66 | | -0.30 | 0.73 |
| Forest | 121 | 27 | 24 | 62 | 0.12 | 0.20 | -0.75 | 0.05 | 0.12 |
| Union Pacific | 87 | 68 | 29 | 29 | 0.07 | 0.24 | -0.08 | -0.27 | -0.16 |
| Odeco | 75 | 12 | 32 | 86 | 0.06 | 0.42 | | -0.31 | 0.16 |
| Enserch | 33 | 60 | 52 | 36 | 0.02 | -0.10 | -0.26 | 0.64 | -0.33 |
| Forcenergy | 54 | 26 | 41 | 63 | 0.01 | -0.58 | 0.94 | 0.45 | -0.73 |
| Phillips | 113 | 89 | 25 | 23 | -0.01 | 0.68 | -0.48 | 0.00 | 0.14 |
| Energy Devel | 44 | 30 | 44 | 58 | -0.04 | 0.20 | 0.27 | -0.43 | -0.06 |
| Umc | 16 | 36 | 79 | 45 | -0.06 | 0.44 | -0.70 | -0.79 | 0.64 |
| Seneca | 41 | 42 | 46 | 42 | -0.07 | 0.28 | | 0.10 | -0.49 |

39

Table 2.12: Top 50 Firms in Either Production or Leases Acquired from 1990 to 1999 Ranked by Z-scores for Average High Bids, with Z-scores for Total, Shallow, Deep, Competitive, and Noncompetitive Average High Bids (continued)

| Company | Production | Leases | Rank | | Z-Score for Average High Bid | | | | |
|---|---|---|---|---|---|---|---|---|---|
| | MMBOE | Number | BOE | Leases | Total | Shallow | Deep | Competitive | Non Competitive |
| Pogo | 44 | 31 | 45 | 55 | -0.13 | -0.46 | 1.78 | -0.16 | -0.36 |
| Apache | 124 | 45 | 23 | 41 | -0.18 | 0.17 | | -0.39 | -0.45 |
| Santa Fe | 62 | 65 | 36 | 30 | -0.19 | -0.14 | -0.16 | -0.63 | 0.09 |
| Samedan | 187 | 104 | 15 | 20 | -0.21 | -0.08 | -0.05 | 0.63 | -0.07 |
| Norcen | 96 | 45 | 27 | 40 | -0.23 | 0.00 | 0.23 | -0.40 | -0.47 |
| Louisiana L&E | 63 | 82 | 35 | 24 | -0.36 | -0.01 | -0.46 | -0.58 | -0.37 |
| Hall-Houston | 84 | 28 | 30 | 61 | -0.37 | -0.03 | | -0.77 | -0.26 |
| Enron | 94 | 115 | 28 | 17 | -0.39 | -0.14 | -0.17 | -0.43 | -0.09 |
| Fina | | 41 | | 43 | -0.39 | -0.15 | -0.43 | -0.81 | -0.07 |
| ARCO | 182 | 109 | 17 | 19 | -0.44 | -0.10 | | -0.12 | -0.58 |
| Seagull | 59 | 89 | 38 | 22 | -0.45 | -0.77 | 5.63 | -0.21 | -0.19 |
| Texaco | 547 | 404 | 5 | 4 | -0.47 | -0.36 | -0.47 | -0.12 | -0.32 |
| Nippon | 5 | 38 | 116 | 44 | -0.54 | -0.45 | -0.08 | -1.08 | -0.01 |
| BP | 315 | 418 | 11 | 3 | -0.56 | -0.03 | -0.55 | -0.20 | -0.28 |
| Chieftain | 2 | 57 | 147 | 37 | -0.59 | -0.36 | 0.22 | -0.30 | -0.85 |
| Shell | 1,579 | 789 | 1 | 1 | -0.62 | -0.30 | -0.56 | -0.29 | -0.41 |
| Petrobras | 4 | 35 | 121 | 46 | -0.62 | -0.46 | -0.36 | -0.71 | -0.69 |
| Conoco | 382 | 268 | 7 | 9 | -0.63 | -1.03 | -0.52 | -0.69 | -0.35 |
| King Ranch | 8 | 34 | 100 | 49 | -0.64 | -0.28 | | -1.11 | -0.40 |
| Nerco | 55 | 15 | 39 | 80 | -0.69 | -0.36 | | -1.10 | -0.16 |
| BHP | 20 | 207 | 68 | 12 | -0.76 | 0.00 | -0.68 | -0.58 | -0.70 |
| Exxon | 595 | 354 | 4 | 5 | -0.80 | -0.02 | -0.66 | -0.51 | -0.53 |
| Amoco | 341 | 243 | 9 | 10 | -0.82 | -0.34 | -0.67 | -0.57 | -0.73 |
| Walter | 159 | 52 | 20 | 39 | -0.83 | -0.51 | -0.61 | -0.85 | -0.59 |
| Sonat | 101 | 64 | 26 | 31 | -0.83 | -0.90 | -0.46 | 0.42 | -0.54 |
| Houston Expl | 37 | 63 | 47 | 33 | -0.91 | -0.58 | -0.84 | -0.50 | -0.87 |
| Chevron | 1,449 | 494 | 2 | 2 | -0.96 | -0.92 | -0.65 | -0.07 | -0.91 |
| Mobil | 629 | 341 | 3 | 7 | -1.01 | -1.17 | -0.64 | -0.78 | -0.74 |
| Pennzoil | 372 | 96 | 8 | 21 | -1.09 | -0.84 | -0.66 | -1.17 | -0.84 |
| Coastal | 69 | 72 | 34 | 27 | -1.09 | -0.76 | -0.74 | -0.95 | -0.77 |
| Newfield | 160 | 33 | 19 | 53 | -1.13 | -0.81 | | -1.38 | -0.85 |
| Cxy | 29 | 62 | 57 | 35 | -1.22 | -0.99 | -0.29 | -1.18 | -1.14 |
| Zilkha | 62 | 348 | 37 | 6 | -1.64 | -1.34 | -0.94 | -1.87 | -1.29 |

40

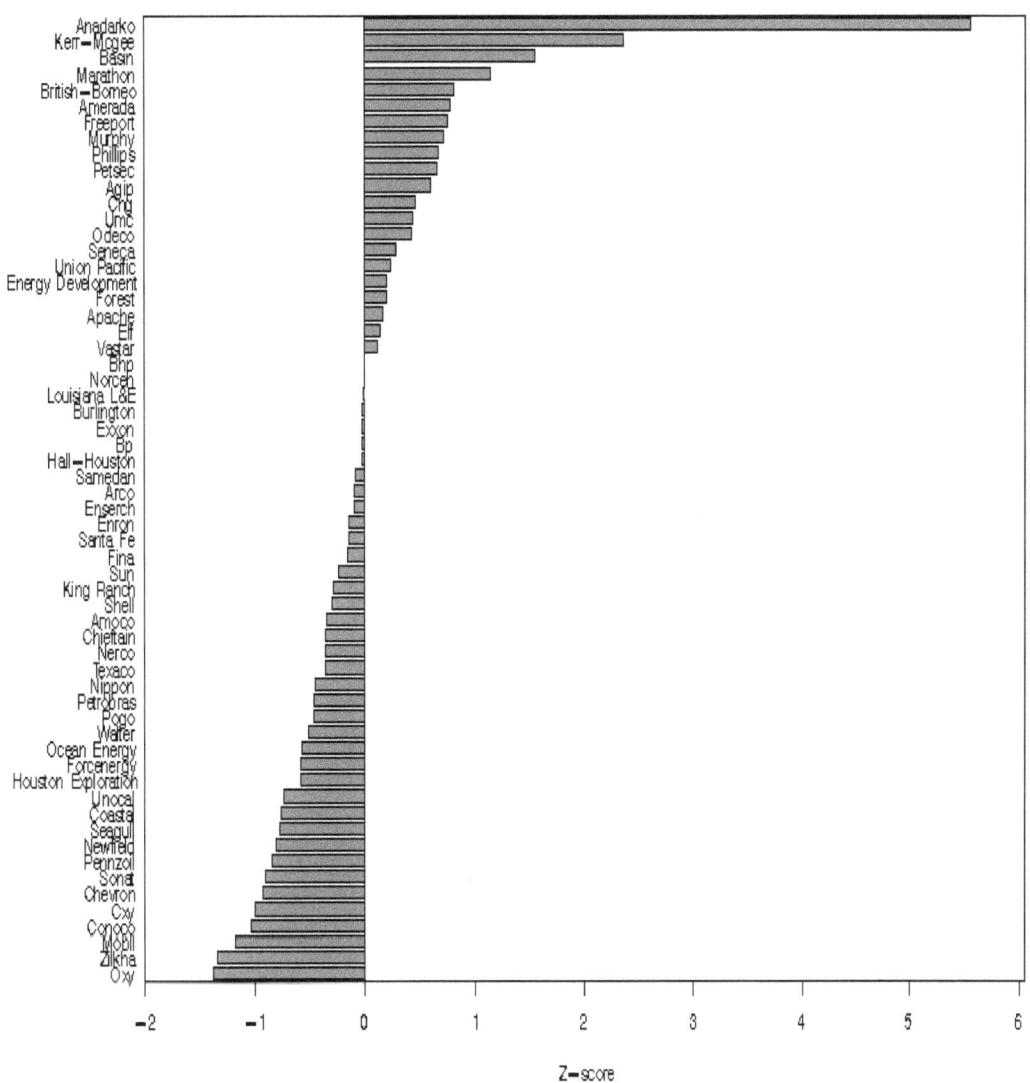

Figure 2.7: Z-Scores for Average High Bids (Shallow Water).

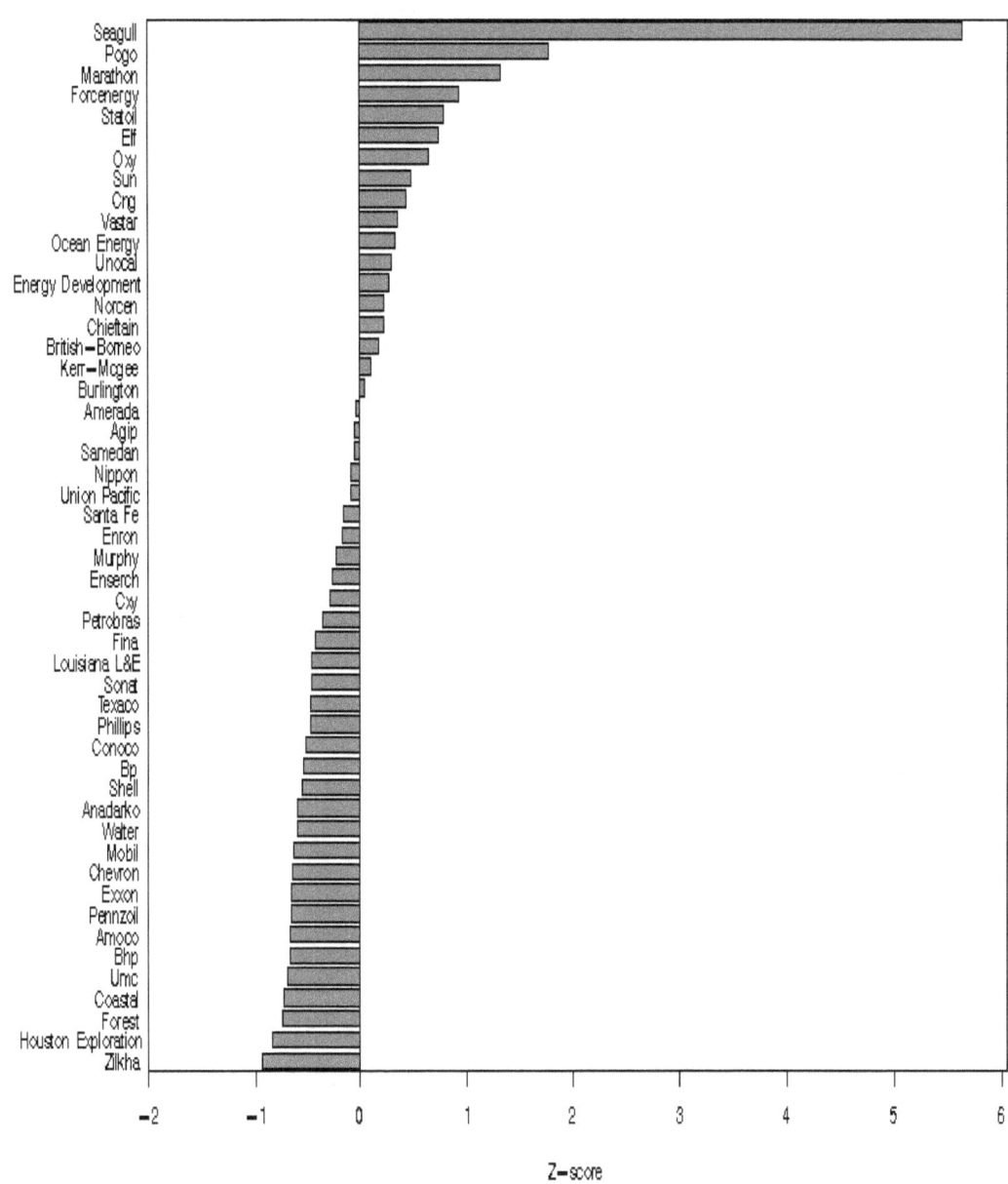

Figure 2.8: Z-Scores for Average High Bids (Deep Water).

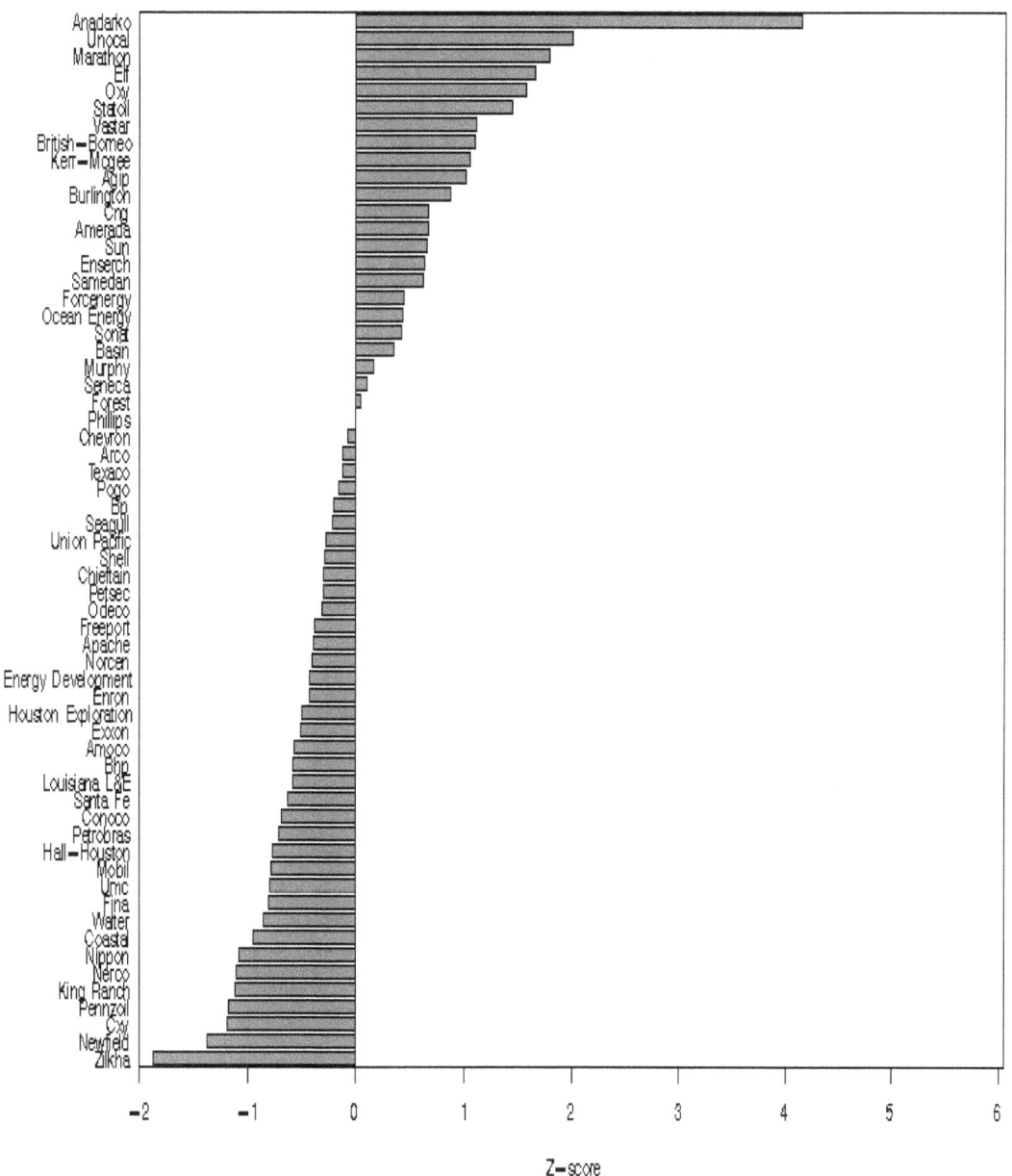

Figure 2.9: Z-Scores for Average High Bids (Competitive Bids).

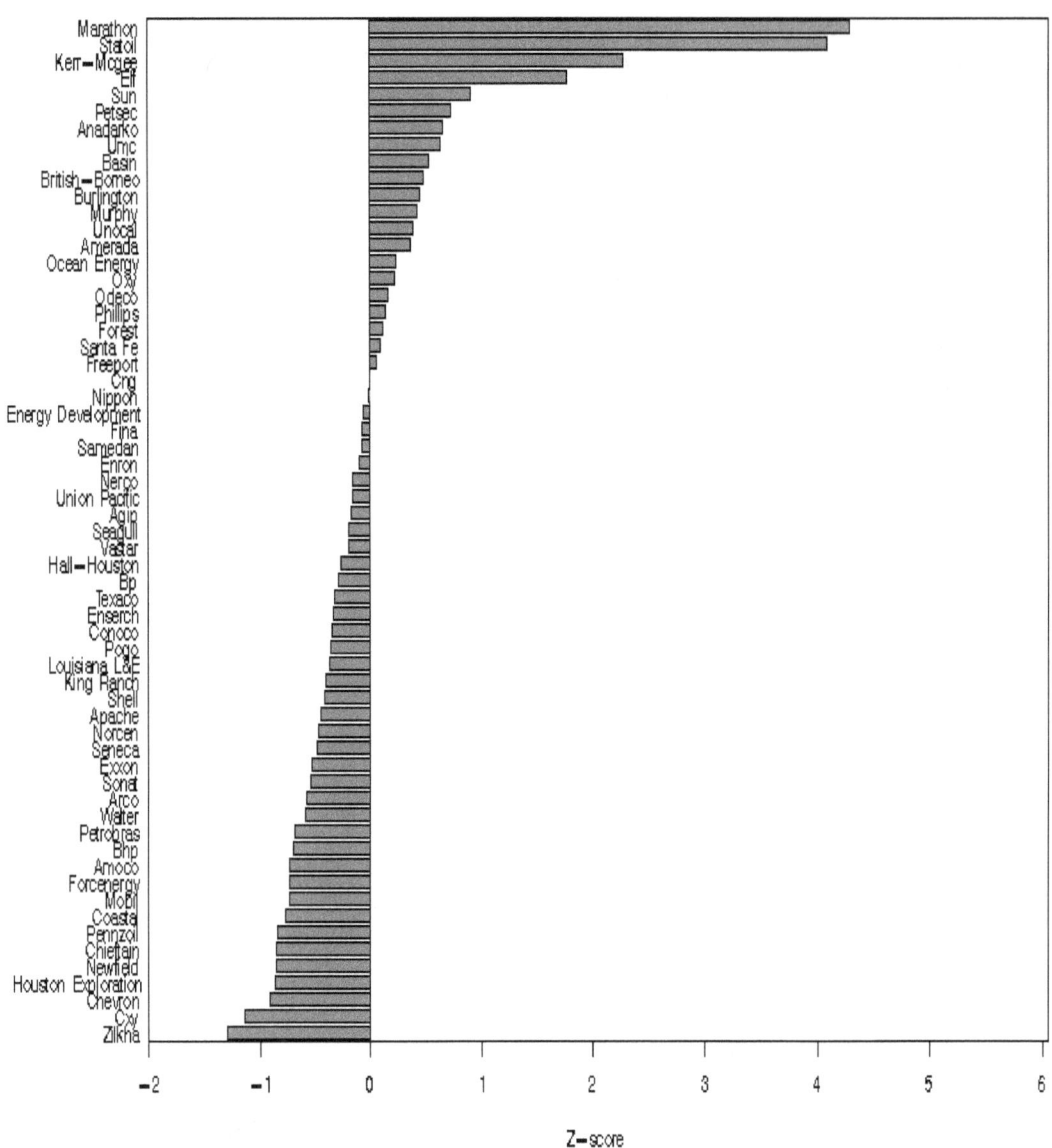

Figure 2.10: Z-Scores for Average High Bids (Single Bids).

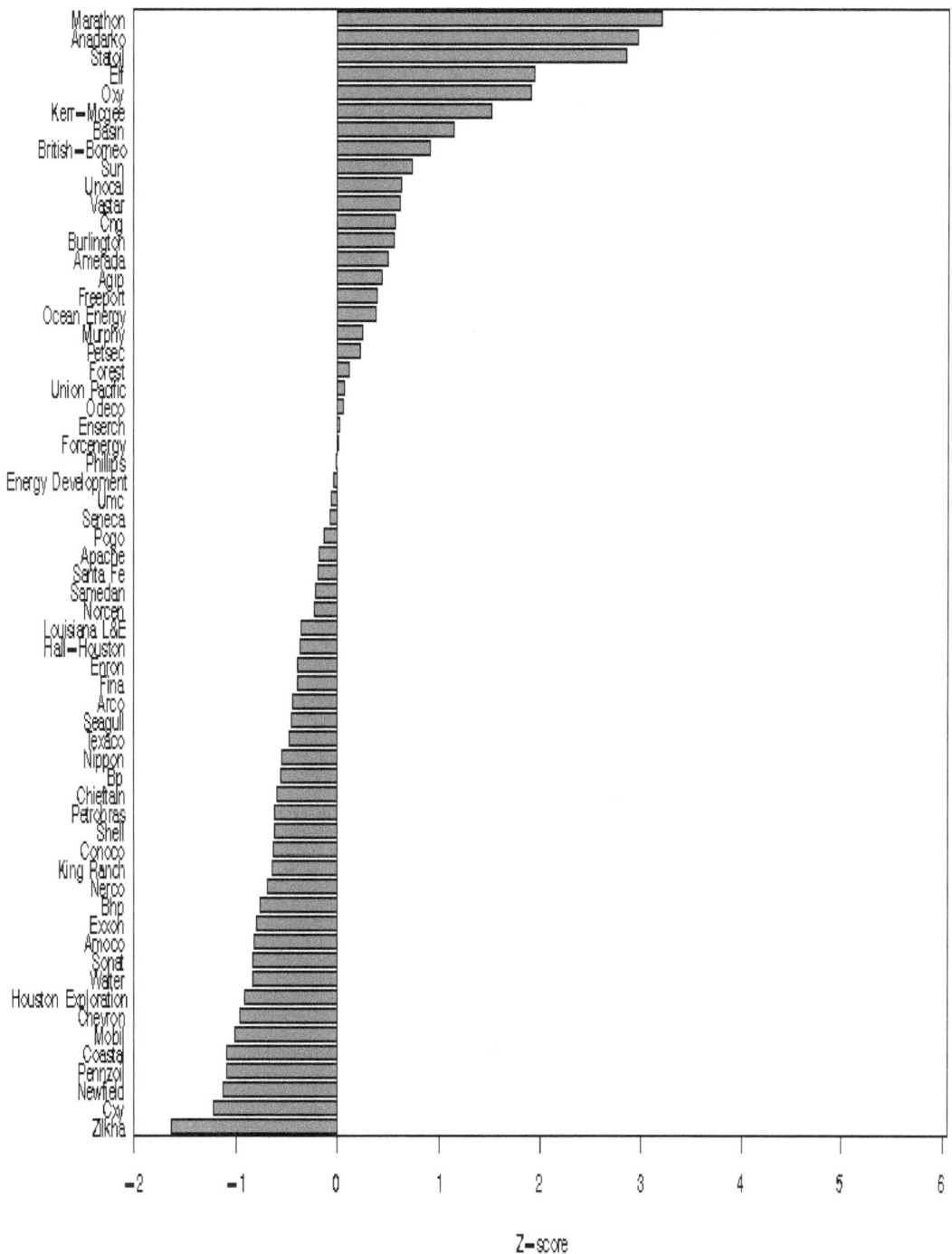

Figure 2.11: Z-Scores for Average High Bids (All Bids).

**Table 2.12** inspires several observations--although all of them need further analysis at a more detailed level.

- The number of firms that appear to bid either higher or lower than the norm is quite small. Keeping in mind that all the observations are winning bids, "high-winning bids," i.e. bids that are significantly higher than the average winning bid, might suggest worse than average bidding ("worse" from the perspective of the shareholders of the bidders but "better" for the government's revenues) and are referred to here as "too-high-winning bids." Conversely "too-low-winning bids" indicate better than average bidding performance from the standpoint of the firm but are, in a similar sense, "too-low" from the standpoint of the government. Using 1.5 standard deviations as an admittedly ad hoc criterion for making such a determination:
    - Six firms, Marathon, Anadarko, Statoil, Elf, Oxy, and Kerr-McGee, might be termed "too-high-winning" bidders and one firm, Zilkha, a "too-low-winning" bidder for all leases considered together.
    - Three firms were "too-high-winning" bidders for shallow leases and two for deep leases. No firm met the criteria for "too-low-winning" bidder in either category.
    - Five firms were "too-high-winning" bidders for competitive leases and four for noncompetitive leases.
    - One firm was a "too-low-winning bidder" for competitive leases and no firms met the criteria for noncompetitive leases.

- Only a few firms appear to meet the criteria for "too-high-winning" bidder or "too-low-winning" bidder consistently:
    - Marathon's average high bid was more than one standard deviation above the mean in each of the five categories and exceeded the 1.5 criteria in three of them.
    - Elf and Kerr-McGee also exceeded the criteria in three of five categories.
    - Anadarko, Statoil and Oxy met fell into the "too-high-winning" bidder category for two of the five series.
    - Zilka was the only firm to earn the more desirable "too-low-winning" bidder it did this in two categories.

- The firms listed on MMS' Restricted Bidders List, discussed later in this chapter, all fall in the lower end of each of the five series, but only Mobil was (barely) more than one standard deviation below the mean in any series.

- The timing of the "leasing-up" of the Deep Gulf may be reflected in the relationships in **Table 2.12**. Larger firms such as those on the Restricted Bidders List dominated lease sales in the 1992-96 period. Participation by smaller majors and larger independents grew significantly in 1997-99 period. If the perception had spread that opportunities to participate in deepwater activity were becoming scarce, average bids may have been elevated later in the period.

### 3. Mergers and Acquisitions, Firm Size and the Market for OCS Leases

Implicit in the concern about possible effects of mergers and acquisitions on the leasing of oil and gas tracts in the Gulf of Mexico is apprehension that firms participating in the process may become large enough to exercise market power for their own advantage. However, mergers and acquisitions are not the only or necessarily most important route to large size. As emphasized previously, the growth of Shell's share of production has been a more quantitatively important factor in changing the structure of the offshore industry output than the mega-mergers. Further, smaller independents have been at least as active participants in merger and acquisition activity as the majors whose mega-mergers have attracted attention in recent years. In other words, merger and acquisition experience and the size of firms are separable characteristics.

The objective in this chapter is to determine whether the attributes of leases won by firms who have a history of mergers and acquisitions and leases won by firms of different sizes are related to the structure, conduct and performance of the market for oil and gas leases in the Gulf of Mexico OCS region.

### 3.1 Effects of Mergers and Acquisitions

This section analyzes the lease records from 1983-1999 to investigate changing patterns of ownership in the E&P industry on the structure, conduct, and performance of the market for oil and gas leases in the Gulf of Mexico OCS region. The primary approach is a descriptive analysis of the data and empirical testing of the differences in the mean values of lease statistics that characterized the OCS lease auction market and the conduct of participating bidders.

To do this, all OCS leases from 1989-1999 were classified into three categories.

> Group A: Leases with high bids (solo or joint) by firms that were not involved in mergers and acquisitions from 1983-1999. This represents the control group in the analysis.

> Group B: Leases won by firms involved in mergers and acquisitions prior to the time of lease sales during the period 1983-1999. Joint ventures leases, which involve other firms without such experience, are also included in this category.

> Group C: Leases with winning bids submitted solely or jointly by firms that were candidates for M&A between 1983-1999, but M&A had not occurred prior to the time of lease sales. As with Group B, joint ventures leases, which involved firms from Group A, were included.

**Table 3.1** presents aggregate statistics on oil and gas leases in the Gulf of Mexico OCS. The summary information is organized by category of leases as described above and by period. Two sub-periods 1983-1989 and 1990-1999 have been selected arbitrarily, but they clearly show major movement among the three categories over the period.

Table 3.1

Aggregate Values of OCS Lease Attributes

| OCS Auction Attributes | Period | Group A | Group B | Group C | Aggregate |
|---|---|---|---|---|---|
| Number of Operators | 1983-89 | 188 | 51 | 92 | 191 |
| | 1990-99 | 222 | 100 | 55 | 223 |
| Percent Change | | 18 | 96 | (40) | 17 |
| Number of Leases | 1983-89 | 4,796 | 145 | 604 | 5,545 |
| | 1990-99 | 7,121 | 1,115 | 165 | 8,401 |
| Percent Change | | 48 | 670 | (73) | 52 |
| Number of Bids | 1983-89 | 6,894 | 213 | 859 | 7,966 |
| | 1990-99 | 10,642 | 1,535 | 218 | 12,395 |
| Percent Change | | 54 | 621 | (75) | 56 |
| Number of Bidders | 1983-89 | 11,455 | 268 | 1,656 | 13,369 |
| | 1990-99 | 14,401 | 2,203 | 291 | 16,895 |
| Percent Change | | 26 | 722 | (82) | 26 |
| Total Bonus Exposed, $MM | 1983-89 | 12,155 | 124 | 2,688 | 14,937 |
| | 1990-99 | 7,207 | 960 | 135 | 8,302 |
| Percent Change | | (69) | 674 | (95) | (44) |
| Total High Bid Bonus, $MM | 1983-89 | 8,796 | 89 | 1,997 | 10,882 |
| | 1990-99 | 5,048 | 681 | 111 | 5,839 |
| Percent Change | | (43) | 665 | (94) | (46) |

More specifically, Group A is the largest category and dominates the aggregate measures over both periods, but its growth is relatively modest. Group B starts from a much smaller relative base, but grows much more dramatically in each attribute category, while, conversely, Group C declines much more dramatically as firms shift from Group C to Group B throughout the period.

The total number of firms[11] that submitted or participated in at least one high bonus bid (joint or solo) for leases on the OCS from 1983 to 1999 was 414. These firms exposed themselves to about $23,240 billion for the right to own and develop 13,946 leases awarded from 1983 to1999. The surrendered cash value of the high bonus bids for the period was $16.721 billion. This represents 72 percent of the total bonus exposed during the period.

From 1983-1989, 191 operators surrendered $10.882 billion for high bonus bids against the total bid bonus value of $14,937 billion (73 percent of total bonus bid value). Whereas the total value of high bonus bids submitted by 223 operators was about $5.839 billion in the period 1990-1999, a decline of nearly 46 percent from the total bonus in the 1980s.

---

[11] The number of "firms" is more precisely, the number of different MMS operator identification numbers assigned to at least one winning bid. Different identification numbers may be assigned to the same commercial entity as a consequence of changes in legal or internal organization of the entity or because of administrative procedures implemented or followed by MMS. All identification numbers associated with the commercial entity are classified consistently in the three groups.

It should be noted that this drop occurred despite the noticeable increase in the number of bids submitted and the expansion in the number of participating bidders. The fraction of the total bid bonus value that was surrendered from 1990 to 1999, in the aggregate, was 70.3 percent, a 2.6 percent drop from what was surrendered from 1983-1989.

**Table 3.2** presents sample statistics measuring the structure, conduct and performance of the market for OCS oil and gas lease sales from 1983-1999. **Table 3.3** shows the same variables for groups A and B separated into the 1983 to 1989 and 1990 to 1999 time periods. The empirical determination of whether there is any difference in two comparable estimates of a random variable requires a specification of two opposing hypotheses: the null hypotheses of interest and the alternative hypothesis. The null hypothesis represents an assumption that ordinary sampling variability does sufficiently explain the observed differences between point estimates of samples drawn from the same population.

The alternative proposition, of course, is that the differences in point estimate cannot be attributed to sample variability but that some other unspecified causes are present. If such a difference is due to the former, then we can conclude that the two estimates are not significantly different, thereby failing to reject the null hypothesis at a given significant level. The significance level provides an estimated probability that the null hypothesis is true and can also mean that the alternative hypothesis is false (Brennan and Caroll, 1987).

Using these statistical concepts on hypotheses and the test of significance of sample statistics, the effects of mergers and acquisitions are analyzed in **Table 3.3** for each of the variables summarized in **Table 3.2**. The null hypothesis is that there is no difference between the value of the variable for Group A and Group B leases. Each hypothesis is empirically tested for verification or negation depending on whether the sample statistics indicate a level of statistical significance. The level of significance before failing to reject the null hypotheses has been specified at five percent, meaning that the chances of the alternative hypothesis being false is set at less than 95 percent.

The pattern apparent in **Table 3.3** is that bids per lease and bidders per lease variables show little consistent, significant difference in either period between Group A and Group B leases. However the financial variables measuring the average value of the high bid and the average amount of "money left on the table," are consistently and significantly larger for the control group (Group A) than for the merger and acquisition group (Group B) in the earlier 1983 to 1989 period. But, the differences between Group A and Group B shrink to statistical insignificance in the later 1990 to 1999 period. As shown in **Table 3.1**, Group B is much smaller than Group A in the 1983 to 1989 period, and increased much more rapidly.

This same pattern of differences between the two groups eroding from the earlier to later period is reflected in **Table 3.4** which compares the frequency of joint bidding in the acquisition of the Group A and Group B leases. Joint venturing was much more commonly used in bidding on leases in Group A in the earlier period, for both bids and winning or high bids, but was used relatively more for Group B leases in the latter period.

49

Table 3.2

Measures of the Competitive Structure, Type of Bid and Value of Mean High Bids for OCS Oil
and Gas Leases by Lease Category Groups A, B and C, 1983-1999

| Variable | Structure | Type | Group A | Group B | Group C | OCS Total |
|---|---|---|---|---|---|---|
| Bids/Lease | Competitive | Joint | 2.78 | 2.87 | 2.75 | 2.78 |
| | | Solo | 2.66 | 2.61 | 2.54 | 2.65 |
| | | All | 2.70 | 2.72 | 2.66 | 2.70 |
| | Aggregate | Joint | 1.63 | 1.55 | 1.65 | 1.63 |
| | | Solo | 1.40 | 1.30 | 1.30 | 1.39 |
| | | All | 1.47 | 1.39 | 1.44 | 1.46 |
| Bidders/Lease | Noncompetitive | Joint | 2.43 | 2.32 | 3.03 | 2.46 |
| | | All | 1.38 | 1.40 | 1.71 | 1.40 |
| | Competitive | Joint | 5.43 | 4.77 | 6.20 | 5.44 |
| | | Solo | 3.48 | 3.19 | 3.74 | 3.47 |
| | | All | 4.23 | 3.89 | 5.13 | 4.26 |
| | Aggregate | Joint | 3.50 | 3.04 | 4.21 | 3.51 |
| | | Solo | 1.60 | 1.41 | 1.53 | 1.58 |
| | | All | 2.16 | 1.96 | 2.62 | 2.17 |
| MLOT/Lease, $ Thousand[a] | Competitive | Joint | 1,636 | 993 | 5,335 | 1,887 |
| | | Solo | 977 | 632 | 1,828 | 989 |
| | | All | 1,230 | 793 | 3,813 | 1,347 |
| High Bonus/Lease, $ Thousand | Noncompetitive | Joint | 1,180 | 547 | 2,048 | 1,177 |
| | | Solo | 611 | 308 | 1,188 | 614 |
| | | All | 761 | 381 | 1,488 | 768 |
| | Competitive | Joint | 2,993 | 1,739 | 7,893 | 3,291 |
| | | Solo | 1,722 | 1,138 | 3,249 | 1,746 |
| | | All | 2,211 | 1,406 | 5,879 | 2,363 |
| | Aggregate | Joint | 1,825 | 901 | 4,225 | 1,920 |
| | | Solo | 879 | 464 | 1,591 | 879 |
| | | All | 1,160 | 611 | 2,662 | 1,199 |

[a]MLOT means the total money left on the table, which measures the difference between the value of the high bonus
bid and the value of the next highest bid for the lease.

Table 3.3

Measures of the Competitive Structure, Type of Bid and Value of Mean High Bids
for OCS Oil and Gas Leases by Lease Category Groups A and B,
1983-1989 and 1990-1999

| Variable | Structure | Type of Bid | 1983-1989 Group A[a] | 1983-1989 Group B | 1990-1999 Group A | 1990-1999 Group B |
|---|---|---|---|---|---|---|
| Bids/Lease | Competitive | Joint | 2.78 | 3.00 | 2.78 | 2.86 |
| | | Solo | 2.54 | 2.82 | 2.71 | 2.56 |
| | | All | 2.65 | 2.84 | 2.73 | 2.71 |
| | Aggregate | Joint | 1.60 | 1.47 | 1.66 | 1.56 |
| | | Solo | 1.34 | 1.47 | 1.44(+) | 1.27 |
| | | All | 1.43 | 1.47 | 1.49 | 1.38 |
| Bidders/Lease | Noncompetitive | Joint | 2.60(-) | 3.23 | 2.25 | 2.27 |
| | | All | 1.52(+) | 1.27 | 1.28(-) | 1.42 |
| | Competitive | Joint | 6.09 | 6.00 | 4.85 | 4.73 |
| | | Solo | 3.65 | 3.24 | 3.39 | 3.18 |
| | | All | 4.80(+) | 3.54 | 3.87 | 3.95 |
| | Aggregate | Joint | 3.78 | 3.88 | 3.21(+) | 3.01 |
| | | Solo | 1.58 | 1.58 | 1.61 | 1.38 |
| | | All | 2.38(+) | 1.85 | 2.01 | 1.98 |
| MLOT/Lease, $ Thousand | Competitive[b] | Joint | 2,410(+) | 831 | 942 | 999 |
| | | Solo | 1,520(+) | 666 | 705 | 623 |
| | | All | 1,940(+) | 684 | 784 | 809 |
| High Bids/Lease, $Thousand | Noncompetitive | Joint | 1,710(+) | 448 | 635 | 551 |
| | | Solo | 974(+) | 396 | 393(+) | 293 |
| | | All | 1,210(+) | 402 | 446 | 378 |
| | Competitive | Joint | 4,500(+) | 1,550 | 1,650 | 1,750 |
| | | Solo | 2,690(+) | 1,190 | 1,240 | 1,120 |
| | | All | 3,540(+) | 1,230 | 1,370 | 1,430 |
| | Aggregate | Joint | 2,660(+) | 708 | 1,010 | 909 |
| | | Solo | 1,350(+) | 602 | 608(+) | 439 |
| | | All | 1,830(+) | 614 | 710 | 610 |

[a] Differences significant at the .95 level for values for Group A and Group B leases are indicated with bold typeface, (+) indicates the Value for A is significantly larger and (-) indicating significantly smaller, regular type face indicates no difference between values for the two groups.
[b] At least two bids are required for any "money to be left on the table."

Table 3.4

Frequency Distribution of Bidding by Joint Venturing

| Type | Bids | Period | Group A | Group B | Group C | Aggregate |
|------|------|--------|---------|---------|---------|-----------|
| All Bids | Total | 1983-89 | 39.7 | 13.6 | 48.3 | 39.9 |
| | | 1990-99 | 26.8 | 33.7 | 21.1 | 27.6 |
| | | | | | | |
| | High | 1983-89 | 36.4 | 11.7 | 43.8 | 36.6 |
| | | 1990-99 | 25.5 | 36.5 | 20.0 | 26.9 |
| Competitive Bids (At Least Two) | | | | | | |
| | Total | 1983-89 | 47.1 | 15.2 | 58.0 | 47.4 |
| | | 1990-99 | 31.0 | 34.8 | 28.1 | 31.4 |
| | | | | | | |
| | High | 1983-89 | 47.0 | 10.8 | 56.8 | 47.1 |
| | | 1990-99 | 33.8 | 49.6 | 33.3 | 35.4 |

**Table 3.5** compares the average value of joint and solo bids among the groups for the two periods we have used in the analysis.

To generalize, the variables we have examined do not show consistent differences between Group A and Group B throughout the time period. Significant differences exist in the earlier period but as Group B grows, they vanish in the latter one.

In summary, the results of the sample means equality testing of the lease attributes reported in **Tables 3.3** and **3.4** point to the following probable effects of mergers and acquisitions on the market for OCS oil and gas leases:

- The effects of M&A on bids per lease (measures of the extent or degree of competition for leases), in the aggregate, were statistically insignificant in the 1980s but highly significant in the 1990s for all leases (noncompetitive and competitive leases).

- M&A did limit significantly the average number of bidders in the 1980s, but no such effect was evident in the 1990s for all leases (noncompetitive and competitive leases).

- The effects of M&A on the mean values of high bids for competitive--solo ventures and joint ventures--leases from 1983-1989 are statistically significant, but insignificant during the 1990-1999 sub-period.

- M&A effects on the mean values of noncompetitive solo ventures are statistically significant in both sub-periods, whereas the effects of M&A on the mean values of high bids for leases that are noncompetitive joint-venture bids in the two sub-periods are insignificant at 95 percent confidence interval.

Table 3.5

Mean Value of High Bids by
Structure, Conduct and Lease Category ($ Million)

| Structure | Conduct | Period | Group A | Group B |
|---|---|---|---|---|
| Competitive | JV | 1983-89 | 4.500 | 1.550 |
| | | 1990-99 | 1.650 | 1.750 |
| | SV | 1983-89 | 2.690 | 1.190 |
| | | 1990-99 | 1.240 | 1.120 |
| | All | 1983-89 | 3.540 | 1.230 |
| | | 1990-99 | 1.370 | 1.430 |
| Noncompetitive | JV | 1983-89 | 1.710 | 0.447 |
| | | 1990-99 | 0.634 | 0.551 |
| | SV | 1983-89 | 0.974 | 0.396 |
| | | 1990-99 | 0.393 | 0.293 |
| | All | 1983-89 | 1.210 | 0.402 |
| | | 1990-99 | 0.446 | 0.377 |

## 3.2 Comparing the Lease Records of Majors and Non-Majors

Oil and gas operators operating in the U.S. Gulf of Mexico are classified for the analysis in this section using the criteria established by the U.S. EIA in its classification of Financial Reporting System (FRS) companies. The major energy companies are designated as majors if they have at least one percent of U.S. crude oil natural gas liquids (NGL) reserves or production, or at least one percent of U.S. natural gas reserves or production (U.S. Dept. of Energy, Energy Information Administration, 2002)[12]. MMS also used a major/non-major classification in some publications, which is more selective than this classification. The majors defined by MMS are basically the firms on its Restricted Bidders List (Shell, Exxon-Mobil, BP-Amoco-Arco, Chevron) plus Texaco.

**Table 3.6** presents the value of lease attributes summarizing the group effects of firms of different sizes on lease market structure and performance from 1983-1999. The columns show the mean values or magnitudes for those leases in which the winning bids were submitted by: 1) majors submitting solo bids or joint bid with other majors, 2) joint bids submitted by groups including both majors and non-majors, and 3) non-majors submitting solo bids or joint bids with other non-majors.

---

[12] The U.S. based companies that respond to the Financial Reporting System (FRS) for EIA-28 in 2000 with operations on the Gulf of Mexico OCS are Arco, BP Amoco, Amerada, Anadarko, Burlington, Chevron, Coastal, Conoco, Diamond, El Paso, Enron, Exxon, Fina, Kerr McGee, Marathon, Mobil, Penzoil, Phillips, Shell, Texaco, Union Pacific, Unocal, Valero, Williams.

Table 3.6

Comparison of OCS Lease Attributes by Structure and Conduct, 1983-1999

| Lease Attributes | Structure | Conduct | Majors | Majors and Non-majors | Non-majors |
|---|---|---|---|---|---|
| Bids/Lease | Competitive | Joint | 2.59 | 2.83 | 2.82 |
| | | Solo | 2.61 | | 2.71 |
| Total Bonus/Lease, $ 000 | Noncompetitive | Joint | 793 | 1,558 | 1,001 |
| | | Solo | 612 | | 617 |
| | Competitive | Joint | 1,392 | 2,867 | 1,293 |
| | | Solo | 1,110 | | 881 |
| Bidders/Lease | Noncompetitive | Joint | 2.09 | 2.54 | 2.61 |
| | Competitive | Joint | 4.57 | 5.97 | 5.39 |
| | | Solo | 3.44 | | 3.51 |
| High Bonus/Lease, $ 000 | Noncompetitive | Joint | 793 | 1,558 | 1,001 |
| | | Solo | 612 | | 617 |
| | Compétitive | Joint | 2,280 | 5,162 | 2,218 |
| | | Solo | 1,923 | | 1,465 |

Data in **Table 3.6** show a higher degree of competition for leases in which non-majors were involved either through joint or solo bidding arrangement than those that involved only majors under the same bidding environment from 1983-1999. Statistical tests of the equality of the means confirmed that the number of bids per lease for leases involving non-major operators (2.83 or 2.82) is significantly greater than for leases involving majors only (2.59) when bidding jointly[13]. The result of the tests also lead to reject the null of hypothesis that when bidding arrangement is by solo ventures, the number of bids per lease involving only majors equal to that involving non-majors only.

There were also more bidders (number of firms participating) per lease for leases involving non-majors irrespective of whether the bids for the leases are competitive or non competitive as long as the bidding arrangement is joint venturing. Testing the significance of the differences in the means of the categories in **Table 3.6**, however, does not confirm the above conjecture when bidding is competitive and the bidding arrangement in the winning bid was a solo venture.

Leases involving majors and non-majors as partners in the high bids for all performance attributes reveal significantly lower mean values when compared with the mean values of the

---

[13] We evaluated the differences between the average performance indicators for restricted and nonrestricted companies using the standard t-test. The null hypothesis is the hypothesis that the means for the two groups are not different, i.e., the difference between the means is not greater than zero, at a given significance level (we used 0.1 or 90% probability). Whenever the null hypothesis is rejected, this indicates that there is an observable statistical difference between the means for the two groups. In the table of the t-test results, negative one (-1) indicates that the mean for the restricted companies is larger than that for the nonrestricted companies, while the positive one (1) indicate the reverse condition.

lease attributes for all categories of leases won by majors or non-major operators. In other words, the value of the high bonus bids for leases involving both majors and non-majors as partners were significantly higher than for leases involving only the majors or non-majors.

Data comparing lease market performance attributes for the two sub-periods for majors and non-majors are presented in **Table 3.7**. In all cases, the expected value of the average bonus per lease, the average money left on the table (MLOT), and that of the high bonus per lease declined significantly in the 1990-99 sub-period relative to the mean values in the 1983-89 periods. The average decline in bonus exposed per lease as well as the average bonus per lease paid in the 1990s by both the majors and non-majors alike and for all possible categories of leases were more than 50 percent the mean values in the 1980s (See **Figure 3.1**). The drastic decline could be attributed to changes in oil and gas market conditions in terms of oil price stability other things being equal. The price of oil was considerably less attractive in the post price crash era in 1986 than they were in the early 1980s. **Figure 3.2** shows the percent change in the high bonus bids by structure and conduct between 1980s to the 1990s.

The average number of bidders per lease won by majors through joint venturing in the 1980s, on average, was 2.97 compared to an average of 2.82 in the 1990s, a drop of about five percent. When all the leases won by non-majors bidding jointly were evaluated, the average number of bidders per lease in the 1980s and the 1990s was 3.84 and 3.62, respectively. This is a decline of about 5.73 percent. However, the number of high bids submitted per lease by major oil and gas producers through joint ventures decreased very marginally by just 1.32 percent in the 1990s from 1.51 in the 1980s. Whereas the number of high bids per lease by non-majors bidding jointly increased by 2.54 percent between the 1980s and 1990s.

Majors on average paid significantly less than non-major operators for noncompetitive solo leases in the 1980s, but majors paid significantly more in the 1990s. However, majors bidding jointly with other majors paid neither significantly more or less than non-major operators bidding jointly for noncompetitive leases in both sub-periods. When leases receiving at least two bids were evaluated, statistical tests of the equality of the means suggested no evidence that majors bidding jointly with other majors paid significantly more or less than non-major operators bidding jointly in both sub-periods. The tests also revealed a statistically significant difference between the bonus the majors and non-majors paid in the 1980s for competitive leases when the bid type is solo venture, but no statistical difference was evident in the 1990s for the same category of leases.

In a statistical sense, the significant differences in lease attributes, between majors as defined in this section, are mixed depending on the classification and bid arrangement for leases, and time period. The values of lease attributes for majors and non-majors are a lot closer in the 1990s than in the 1980s.

Table 3.7

Comparison of OCS Lease Attributes by Structure, Conduct, and Period[a]

| Variable | Structure | Conduct | 1983-1989 | | 1990-1999 | |
|---|---|---|---|---|---|---|
| | | | Majors | Non-Majors | Majors | Non-Majors |
| Bids/lease | Competitive | Joint | 2.46$^{(-)}$ | 2.83 | 2.66 | 2.82 |
| | | Solo | 2.50 | 2.64 | 2.67 | 2.74 |
| | | All | 2.50$^{(-)}$ | 2.73 | 2.66 | 2.77 |
| | Aggregate | Joint | 1.51 | 1.60 | 1.49$^{(-)}$ | 1.82 |
| | | Solo | 1.32 | 1.39 | 1.38$^{(-)}$ | 1.47 |
| | | All | 1.34$^{(-)}$ | 1.47 | 1.39$^{(-)}$ | 1.57 |
| Bidders/Lease | Noncompetitive | Joint | 2.07$^{(-)}$ | 2.78 | 2.09$^{(-)}$ | 2.45 |
| | | All | 1.09$^{(-)}$ | 1.66 | 1.15$^{(-)}$ | 1.35 |
| | Competitive | Joint | 4.65$^{(-)}$ | 6.01 | 4.53$^{(-)}$ | 5.06 |
| | | Solo | 3.57 | 3.88 | 3.36 | 3.37 |
| | | All | 3.74$^{(-)}$ | 4.91 | 3.58$^{(-)}$ | 4.06 |
| | Aggregate | Joint | 2.97$^{(-)}$ | 3.84 | 2.82$^{(-)}$ | 3.62 |
| | | Solo | 1.55 | 1.68 | 1.53$^{(-)}$ | 1.64 |
| | | All | 1.69$^{(-)}$ | 2.55 | 1.73$^{(-)}$ | 2.23 |
| MLOT/Lease, $000 | Competitive | Joint | 2,073 | 1,647 | 997 | 837 |
| | | Solo | 1,728$^{(+)}$ | 1,172 | 767$^{(+)}$ | 607 |
| | | All | 1,780 | 1,401 | 810 | 702 |
| High Bonus/Lease, $000 | Noncompetitive | Joint | 1,344 | 1,364 | 587 | 676 |
| | | Solo | 907$^{(-)}$ | 1,224 | 419$^{(+)}$ | 325 |
| | | All | 944$^{(-)}$ | 1,276 | 442 | 410 |
| | Competitive | Joint | 3,825 | 3,389 | 1,553 | 1,592 |
| | | Solo | 2,957$^{(+)}$ | 2,292 | 1,300 | 1,137 |
| | | All | 3,090 | 2,822 | 1,348 | 1,324 |
| | Aggregate | Joint | 2,208 | 2,026 | 875 | 1,088 |
| | | Solo | 1,342 | 1,475 | 619 | 545 |
| | | All | 1,428$^{(+)}$ | 1,696 | 657 | 705 |

[a] Significant differences in lease attributes at 95 percent level for leases involving any major firm are indicated accordingly in the table using (+) or (-) superscripted signs. (+) indicates the mean value for majors is significantly larger and (-) indicates the value is significantly smaller than the mean value for leases involving non-majors only.

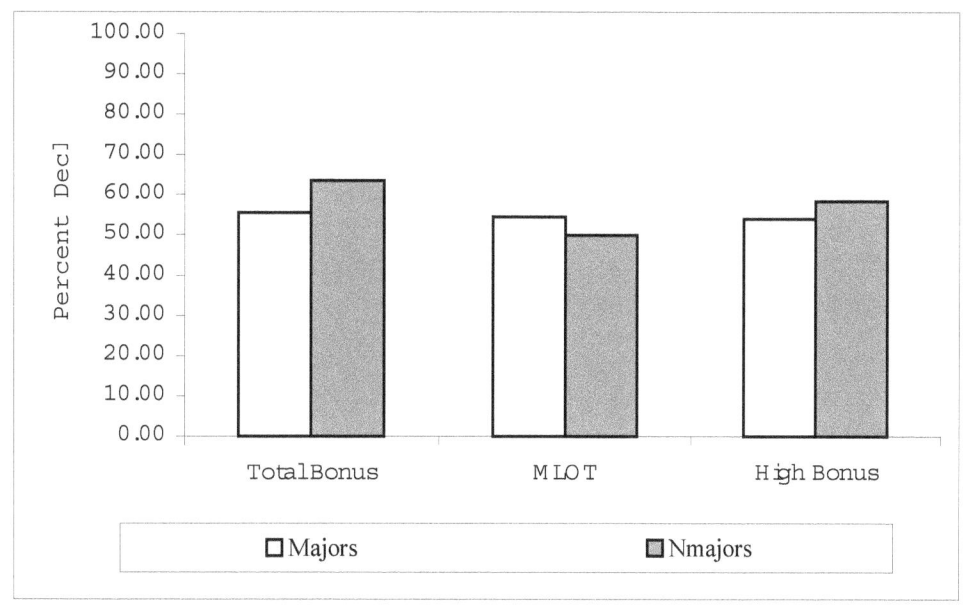

Figure 3.1: Percent Decline in Aggregate Lease Market Performance Attributes Between the 1980s and 1990s.

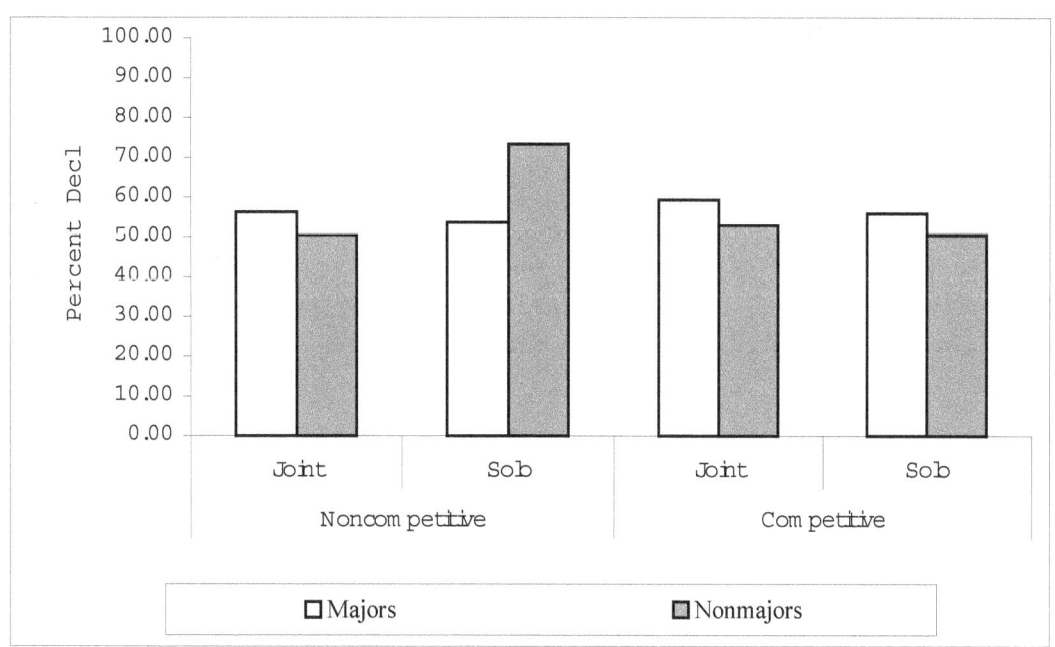

Figure 3.2: Percent Decline in Average High Bonus Bids by Lease Structure and Conduct Between the 1980s and 1990s.

### 3.3 The Restricted Joint Bidders and OCS Lease Market

The principal MMS policy or regulation intended to promote competition (or inhibit collusion) in the lease market is the Restricted Joint Bidders List. It is compiled and published twice a year and applies to all lease sales held during the subsequent six-month period or until the next list is issued. The Energy Policy Conservation Act that was enacted in 1976 requires the list. Relevant provisions in the Act ban companies whose global petroleum production is in excess of 1.6 million barrels of oil equivalent per day from submitting bids jointly in federal OCS lease sales (Moody and Kruvant, 1988; Sullivan et al., 1980).[14]

The list of restricted joint bidders is published in the U.S. Federal Register. **Table 3.8** shows the companies listed since 1983.[15] The table indicates the principal firm and the Roman numeral assigned by MMS when the list was published. Mergers or acquisitions among firms listed are indicated by the use of the same numeral. Thus, after 1999, the merger between Mobil and Exxon, who had been numerals ▯▯▯and ▯respectively, is indicated by assigning Numeral ▯to both firms. Within the parentheses in each cell in the table is the percentage share of Gulf of Mexico production measured in oil equivalent for the year in question.

▯ ▯▯▯▯ ▯▯▯▯▯▯▯▯▯▯▯▯▯▯▯ ▯▯▯ ▯▯▯▯▯▯▯▯Comparing the shares of Gulf production in **Table 3.8** suggests that using global production to determine the restricted bidders results in a different list than if production in the Gulf of Mexico were to be used. Texaco, for example, dropped off the list in 1989 apparently because its global production fell below the 1.6 million barrel floor. However in the Gulf of Mexico, Texaco's production was three or four times as large as British Petroleum's, which appeared on the list beginning in 1988. Similarly, Conoco, which is the fourth largest cumulative producer in the Gulf (see **Figure 2.1** above), and was a top-5 producer during the 1970s and 1980s, never has been listed as a restricted bidder.

Traditional practice and theory in dealing with anti-trust or monopolistic concerns is to apply the analysis to the relevant market or region in which the competition takes place. As a recent study of mergers in the refining industry said, "As its decision to approve the Phillips Tosco merger indicates, the FTC [Federal Trade Commission] focuses on conditions in specific geographic markets, not national concentration statistics. Any assessment of the impact of recent mergers on competition must also consider regional impacts rather than simply changes in national aggregates."[16]

---

[14] The Act, apparently, does not prohibit firms on list from joint operations, only joint bidding. If a firm on the list wants to acquire a share of a lease which is owned or partly owned by another firm also on the list, it makes a request to MMS to do so which MMS forwards to the U.S. Department of Justice for review. According to MMS personnel, such requests are neither very frequent nor extremely rare occurrences, but those that we talked with did not recall any such requests being denied by MMS or the Department of Justice.

[15] Subsidiaries registered under different names, usually identifiable, are listed in the notices in the ▯▯▯▯▯▯▯▯▯▯▯▯ The listing in the table includes all those listed.

[16] Petroleum Industry Research Foundation, ▯▯▯▯▯▯ ▯▯▯▯▯▯▯▯▯▯▯ ▯▯▯ ▯▯▯▯▯▯▯ ▯ ▯▯▯ ▯▯▯NY: 2002, p.3.

Table 3.8

List of Restricted Joint Bidders 1983 to 2001:
Category and Share of Total Gulf of Mexico Production

| Firm/ Period | Chevron | Exxon | Mobil | Shell | BP | Amoco | Vastar | Texaco |
|---|---|---|---|---|---|---|---|---|
| 5/1/01 | V | I | I | II | III | III | III | |
| 11/1/00 | (9.9) | I (7.0) | I | II (21.2) | III (10.5) | III | III | (3.4) |
| 5/1/00 | | I | I | II | III | III | | |
| 11/1/99 | (9.7) | I (4.1) | III (2.0) | II (19.8) | IV (7.8) | IV | (3.2) | (3.7) |
| 5/1/99 | | I | III | II | IV | | | |
| 11/1/98 | (9.9) | I (4.4) | III (3.2) | II (18.0) | IV (3.9) | (3.1) | (2.8) | (4.2) |
| 5/1/98 | | I | III | II | IV | | | |
| 11/1/97 | (10.2) | I (5.2) | III (3.8) | II (15.1) | IV (2.2) | (3.0) | (2.5) | (4.5) |
| 5/1/97 | | I | III | II | IV | | | |
| 11/1/96 | (10.0) | I (5.3) | III (4.7) | II (14.0) | IV (2.0) | (3.1) | (2.8) | (4.9) |
| 5/1/96 | | I | III | II | IV | | | |
| 11/1/95 | (10.7) | I (5.3) | II (5.5) | II (13.3) | IV (1.7) | (3.1) | (3.1) | (4.6) |
| 5/1/95 | | I | III | II | IV | | | |
| 11/1/94 | I (12.2) | II (5.9) | IV (6.1) | III (11.2) | V (1.4) | (3.3) | (2.5) | (4.6) |
| 5/1/94 | I | II | IV | III | V | | | |
| 11/1/93 | I (13.2) | II (5.1) | IV (6.5) | III (10.1) | V (1.5) | (3.6) | | (4.8) |
| 5/1/93 | I | II | IV | III | V | | | |
| 11/1/92 | I (14.5) | II (4.8) | IV (6.8) | III (10.0) | V (1.3) | (3.2) | | (4.7) |
| 5/1/92 | I | II | IV | III | V | | | |
| 11/1/91 | I (14.6) | II (5.2) | IV (6.9) | III (9.0) | V (1.3) | (3.2) | | (5.0) |
| 5/1/91 | I | II | IV | III | V | | | |
| 11/1/90 | I (16.0) | II (5.8) | IV (5.6) | III (8.2) | V (1.9) | (3.3) | | (4.9) |
| 5/1/90 | I | II | IV | III | V | | | |
| 11/1/89 | I (13.6) | II (6.9) | IV (7.8) | III (9.4) | V (1.2) | (3.8) | | (4.7) |
| 5/1/89 | I | II | IV | III | V | | | |
| 11/1/88 | I (10.9) | II (7.0) | V (7.0) | IV (10.4) | VI (0.9) | (3.8) | | III (5.3) |
| 5/1/88 | I | II | V | IV | | | | III |
| 11/1/87 | I (11.2) | II (6.8) | V (6.3) | IV (12.2) | (0.6) | (3.3) | | III (4.8) |
| 5/1/87 | I | II | V | IV | | | | III |
| 11/1/86 | I (11.5) | II (7.6) | V (4.8) | IV (13.1) | (0.3) | (3.1) | | III (5.8) |
| 5/1/86 | I | II | V | IV | | | | III |
| 11/1/85 | I (11.6) | II (7.6) | V (4.2) | IV (12.2) | (0.3) | (2.7) | | III (7.0) |
| 5/1/85 | I | II | III | V | | | | IV |
| 11/1/84 | I (11.8) | II (7.2) | III (4.5) | V (11.5) | (0.1) | (2.5) | | IV (6.5) |
| 5/1/84 | I | II | III | V | | | | IV |
| 11/1/83 | I (12.3) | II (6.7) | III (5.0) | V (12.7) | | (2.4) | | IV (5.6) |
| 5/1/83 | I | II | III | V | | | | IV |

Chevron was not listed between 1995 and 2001 despite the fact that it had been the largest Gulf producer in 1995 and was the second largest producer during the 1995 to 2000 period. Company reports indicate that Chevron's global production exceeded the 1.6 million barrel floor and its absence from the list appears to be the result of a reporting or clerical mix-up. Further, not being listed as a restricted bidder does not appear to have affected its joint-bidding behavior. Only one joint-bid (made with BP in 1996), appears to have been submitted, which would have not been permitted were Chevron listed on the Restricted Bidders List. However, the fact that the mix-up persisted for five years suggests the list has not played a major role in lease sales or bidding for either the firms or the agency.

The potential relative importance of the Restricted Bidders List can be measured by comparing the number of high bids made and bonuses paid by those on the list and the number of high joint bids and bonuses paid to the respective totals for all firms over the period.[17]

- Of the 13,946 leases awarded between 1983 and 1999, 6,554 or about 47 percent went to those firms on the Restricted Bidders List. Of those leases, 1,915 or about 14 percent involved joint bids with other firms.

- The bonus paid for leases won by firms on the restricted list bidding jointly with others was $1.955 billion, which was about 12 percent of the $16,721 billion of total bonuses paid for leases.

Total bonuses paid by restricted bidders amounted to $5,982 billion so joint bids accounted for about 33 percent of their bonus payments.

It is speculative to estimate how many more joint bids and, potentially, fewer competitive bids would have resulted if the Restricted Bidders List were not in force; however, clearly the restricted bidders are a very important part of the lease market and their use of joint bids even under the joint bidder restrictions is not negligible.

**Figure 3.3** illustrates the year-to-year changes in the share of Gulf of Mexico production for the firms on the Restricted Bidders List from 1982 - 2001.

The effects of the Exxon/Mobil and BP/Amoco/ARCO (Vastar) mergers can be clearly seen.

- Before the merger, BP's share had been growing steadily, but after its merger with Amoco it jumped from 5.2 to 7.8 percent in 1999.

- When BP acquired ARCO and its E&P subsidiary Vastar, BP's share increased to 10.5 percent making it the second largest producer in the Gulf.

- Exxon and Mobil both experienced declining production shares prior to their merger and the post merger increase for Exxon/Mobil was more modest—4.1 to 7 percent.

---

[17] For our analysis and exposition we include all firms that were listed as restricted bidders during the period even though some such as Amoco, Chevron, and Texaco were not on the list for the all of the years in period.

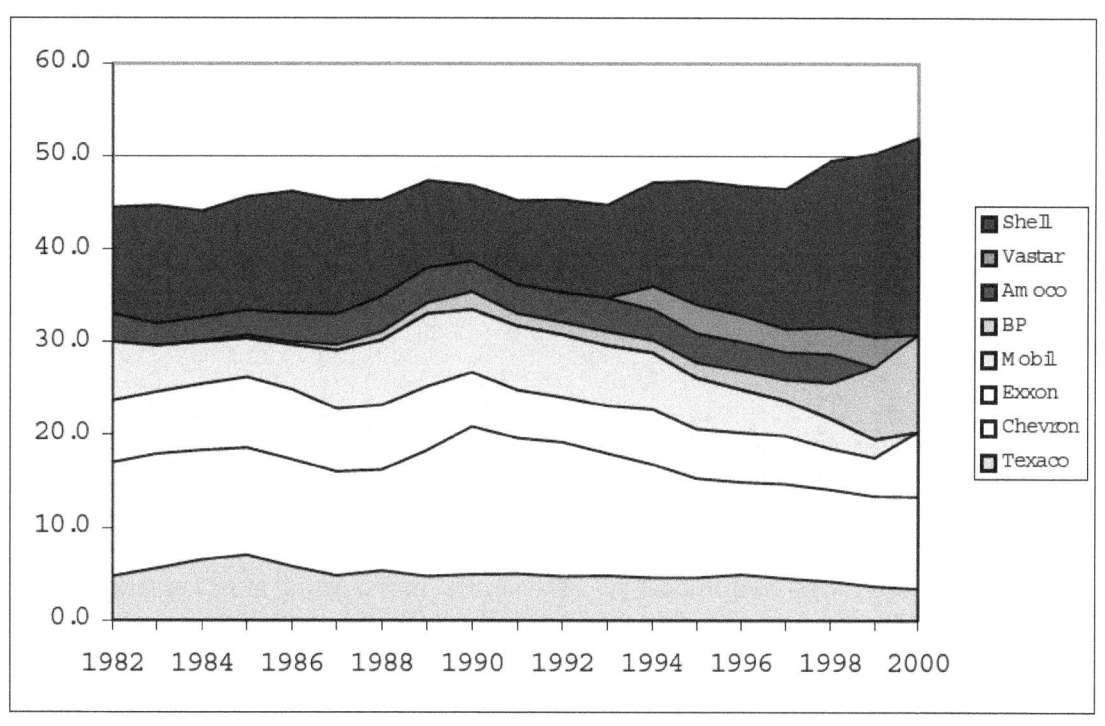

Figure 3.3: Share of GOM Production by MMS' Restricted Joint Bidders, 1982-2000.

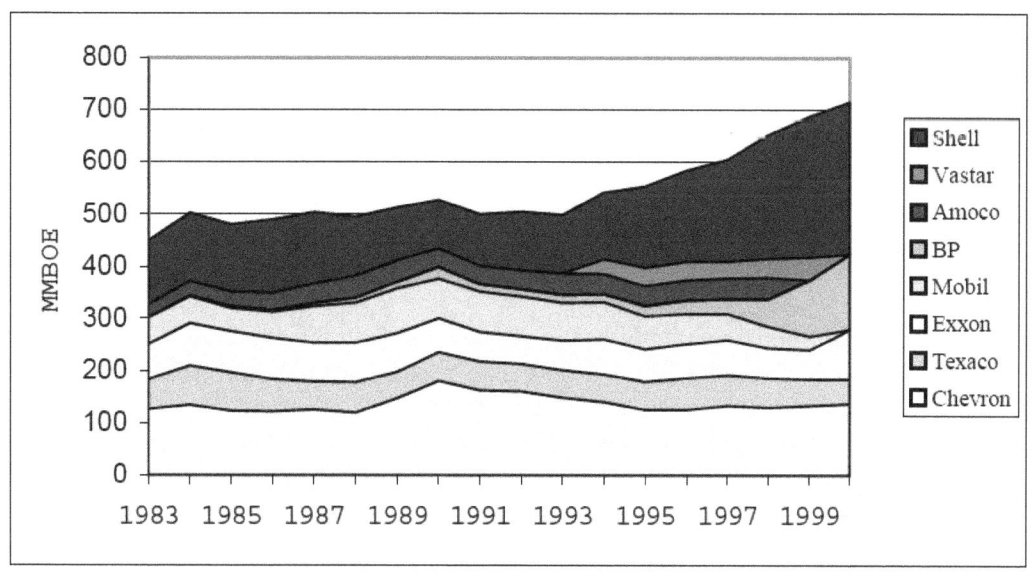

Figure 3.4: Total Production for MMS' Restricted Bidders in the GOM, 1983-2000.

Although changes in production shares of this magnitude warrant analysis, it is important to keep an accurate sense of scale. In a relative sense, changes in the shares of BP/Amoco/Vastar and Exxon/Mobil are dominated by the doubling of Shell's share from about 10 to 20 percent of Gulf production over the period, also illustrated in **Figure 3.3**. As its share of Gulf production nearly doubled from 11.5 to 21.2 percent, its absolute production increased from 120.796 to 292.129 million barrels. Without the mergers, the production levels of the other restricted bidders were stable or were declining. **Figure 3.3** presents the trend in total petroleum production for MMS' restricted joint bidders from 1983-1999.

Thus, both of the major mergers observable resulted in much less concentration of production than did the payoff from non-merger-participant Shell's very successful investment in the deep Gulf.

Looking at the behavior of the restricted joint bidders individually also helps characterize the lease market. **Table 3.9** shows the number and the value of the joint bids won by the restricted bidders and other Gulf of Mexico OCS producers with whom they submitted ten or more bids during the study period.

- Texaco was the most frequent partner in joint bids, participating in 225 winning bids during the period.

- Conoco (207), Amoco (197), Chevron (148) and Unocal (132) were the other members of the five most frequent joint winning bidders.

- Conoco was the only firm to partner with each of the restricted bidders.

- Amoco submitted joint winning bids with all of the restricted bidders except their eventual merger mate BP, and Elf, although only participating in 50 winning bids, partnered with every firm except Texaco.

- Several firms, such as AGIP, Apache, Ensearch, Marathon and Phillips participated in joint bidding primarily with a single firm.

**Figure 3.5** illustrates the major differences in the relative use of joint bids among the firms appearing on the Restricted Bidders List.

- BP, Exxon and Shell use joint bids less extensively than the average.
    - Only 12.5 percent of BP's high bids were made jointly and bonuses paid with those bids amounted to less than 10 percent of BP's total.
    - For Exxon, the comparable percentages were about 25 percent for high bids and 19 percent for bonuses paid.
    - Of Shell's market-leading 1,824 high bids only about 15 percent were made jointly and bonuses paid with those bids amounted to about 22 percent of the firm's total.

Table 3.9

Number of High Joint Bids by Firms on the Restricted
Bidders List and Other Firms: 1983 to 1999

| Amoco | BP | Chevron | Exxon | Mobil | Shell | Texaco | Vastar |
|---|---|---|---|---|---|---|---|
| Shell-71 | BHP-58 | Texaco-136 | Amoco-55 | Phillips-69 | FL Explor.-84 | Chevron-136 | Texaco-17 |
| Exxon-55 | Conoco-12 | BHP-28 | Conoco-48 | Sohio-35 | Flour-84 | Unocal-92 | Elf-15 |
| Tenneco-45 | | Samedan-25 | Sohio-20 | Amoco-32 | Conoco-79 | Uni.Explor-55 | |
| Texaco-32 | | Unocal-20 | Getty-18 | Kerr-McGee-27 | Apache-72 | Pogo-42 | |
| Mobil-32 | | Kerr-McGee-18 | Amerada-18 | Ensearch-18 | Amoco-71 | Amoco-32 | |
| Conoco-19 | | Bechtel-10 | Elf-16 | Agip-13 | Texaco-29 | Conoco-31 | |
| Sun-18 | | | Aminoil-12 | NW Mutual-11 | | Marathon-29 | |
| Pennzoil-18 | | | | Texaco-11 | | Shell-29 | |
| Brit.-Borneo-13 | | | | | | Tricentral-27 | |
| Elf-10 | | | | | | Brit.-Borneo-20 | |
| | | | | | | Samedan-17 | |
| | | | | | | Vastar-17 | |
| | | | | | | Mobil-11 | |
| | | | | | | Getty-10 | |

Note: From lease sale summaries, only firms with ten or more joint bids with a restricted bidder
reported.

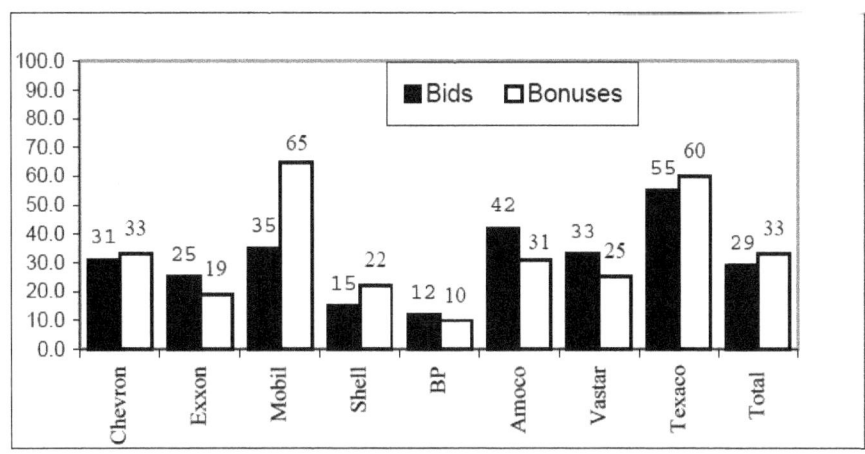

Figure 3.5: Percent of JV High Bids and JV Bonuses for MMS' Restricted
Bidders, 1983-2000.

- Both Chevron and Mobil were close to the average for the group in terms of the proportion of the their bids that were made jointly, but for Mobil bonuses paid with joint bids amounted to 66 percent of the total bonuses they paid, higher than any other firm on the list.

- Amoco and Texaco are of special interest because they were restricted bidders for relatively short increments of the 1983 to 1999 period--one year for Amoco and six for Texaco. When not on the list they were free to, and did, bid jointly with the firms listed. Both firms were large and significant participants in the lease market throughout the study period.
  - Amoco was second only to Texaco with about 42 percent of its high bids made jointly, but was below the average for the group in terms of bonuses paid at 31 percent.
  - Texaco led the group in the proportion of joint bids with about 56 percent and was second to Mobil in bonuses paid at 60 percent.
  - Although an active joint bidder, Amoco had partnered neither with BP nor Vastar prior to their merger.

- Texaco and Chevron, in contrast to BP and Amoco, had an extensive record of joint bidding that closely preceded their merger.
  - Texaco, prior to their merger, cooperated with Chevron in 163 joint bids, of which 136 were winning bids. This amounted to about 28 percent of Texaco's total of 493 joint winning bids.
  - Further, all of the joint Texaco/Chevron bids took place in the last four years of the study period with 158 of the 163 bids submitted during the three sales held in 1996 and 1997.

Many considerations of technology, strategy and corporate planning, globally as well as in the Gulf of Mexico, may have influenced the Chevron/Texaco merger decision, but this episode of collaboration is notable.

**Figure 3.6** shows the location of Texaco/Chevron's joint bids for the lease sales held in the 1996 through 1999 period. It suggests that the bids made at the 1996-1997 sales were distinct initiatives. Most of the bids in 1998 and 1999, in contrast, appear to be efforts to fill-in or expand lease holdings from earlier sales.

The two sales in 1996 and the sale in 1997 were the first wave of the "leasing-up" of the Deepwater Gulf. In 1995 1,012 leases in water depth of 800 meters or more were in effect. In 1996 that number increased to 1,491 and in 1997 to 3,002—a nearly three-fold increase. Further, by 2001, deepwater-leases had only increased to 3,424 (Baud et al., 2002).

The desire to broaden their participation in this "leasing-up" of the deepwater Gulf of Mexico, may have been a causal factor in Chevron/Texaco joint-bidding offensive. There may also have been an element of "catch-up" or "keep-up" involved as well.

**Table 3.10** presents lease attributes summarizing the group effects of MMS' joint bidding restrictions on lease market structure and performance from 1983-1999.

The columns show the mean values or magnitudes for those leases in which the winning bids were submitted by: 1) restricted bidders bidding solo or joint with other non restricted bidders and 2) non restricted bidders submitting solo bids or joint bids with other non restricted bidders in two sub-periods 1983-1989 and 1990-1999, and the entire period, 1983-1999.

The degree of competition measured in terms of bid per lease or bidders per lease as reflected in **Table 3.10** was less in the 1990s for leases in which restricted bidders were involved than when nonrestricted bidders were involved. Also in the 1990s, the value of high bonus per lease was significantly less for leases won by restricted bidders than for those won by non restricted bidders, irrespective of whether the bidding structure is competitive or non competitive. And for all categories of lease structure and bidding arrangement, there is no statistical evidence to suggest that average money left on the table (MLOT) per lease involving restricted bidders is different from MLOT for not involving the other group.

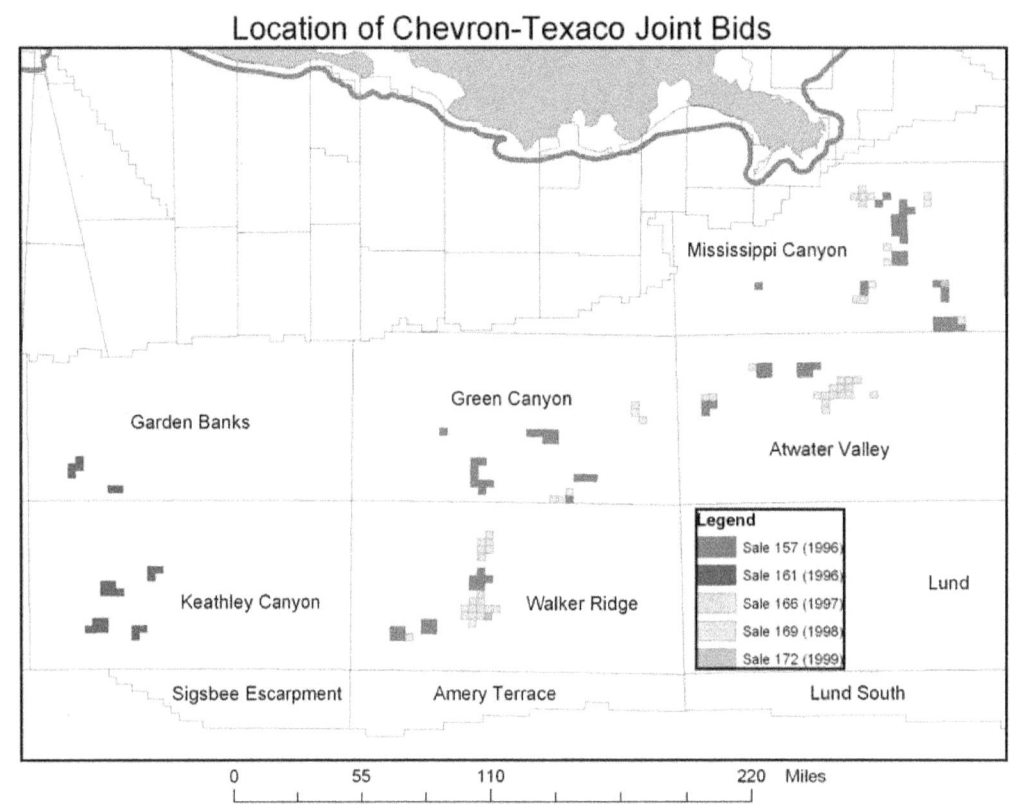

Figure 3.6: Location of Texaco/Chevron's Joint Bids, 1996-1999.

# Table 3.10

## Lease Attributes for Restricted and Unrestricted Bidders[a]

| Variable | Structure | Conduct | 1983-1989 | | 1990-1999 | | 1983-1999 | |
|---|---|---|---|---|---|---|---|---|
| | | | Restricted | Non-Restricted | Restricted | Non-Restricted | Restricted | Non-Restricted |
| Bids/Lease | Competitive | Joint | 2.86 | 2.76 | $2.49^{(-)}$ | 2.80 | 2.77 | 2.79 |
| | | Solo | $2.40^{(-)}$ | 2.64 | $2.53^{(-)}$ | 2.75 | $2.47^{(-)}$ | 2.72 |
| | | All | 2.59 | 2.70 | $2.52^{(-)}$ | 2.77 | $2.56^{(-)}$ | 2.75 |
| | Aggregate | Joint | 1.62 | 1.60 | $1.26^{(-)}$ | 1.72 | $1.48^{(-)}$ | 1.67 |
| | | Solo | $1.25^{(-)}$ | 1.41 | $1.29^{(-)}$ | 1.46 | $1.27^{(-)}$ | 1.45 |
| | | All | $1.35^{(-)}$ | 1.49 | $1.29^{(-)}$ | 1.54 | $1.32^{(-)}$ | 1.53 |
| Bidders/Lease | Noncompetitive | Joint | $2.60^{(-)}$ | 2.70 | $2.09^{(-)}$ | 2.31 | $2.38^{(-)}$ | 2.49 |
| | | All | $1.38^{(-)}$ | 1.68 | $1.20^{(-)}$ | 1.34 | $1.29^{(-)}$ | 1.46 |
| | Competitive | Joint | 6.24 | 6.13 | $4.06^{(-)}$ | 4.90 | 5.70 | 5.38 |
| | | Solo | $3.41^{(-)}$ | 3.84 | $3.08^{(-)}$ | 3.45 | $3.24^{(-)}$ | 3.56 |
| | | All | 4.57 | 4.99 | $3.25^{(-)}$ | 4.02 | $3.97^{(-)}$ | 4.35 |
| | Aggregate | Joint | 3.80 | 3.87 | $2.44^{(-)}$ | 3.35 | $3.28^{(-)}$ | 3.58 |
| | | Solo | $1.44^{(-)}$ | 1.72 | $1.40^{(-)}$ | 1.65 | $1.42^{(-)}$ | 1.67 |
| | | All | $2.09^{(-)}$ | 2.64 | $1.58^{(-)}$ | 2.16 | $1.84^{(-)}$ | 2.33 |
| MLOT/Lease, $000 | Competitive | Joint | $4,705^{(+)}$ | 2,316 | 936 | 923 | $3,773^{(+)}$ | 1,465 |
| | | Solo | 1,650 | 1,483 | 614 | 726 | 1,097 | 946 |
| | | All | $2,897^{(+)}$ | 1,903 | 667 | 804 | $1,899^{(+)}$ | 1,170 |
| High Bonus/Lease, $000 | Noncompetitive | Joint | 2,001 | 1,685 | $332^{(-)}$ | 691 | 1,280 | 1,140 |
| | | Solo | $807^{(-)}$ | 1,187 | 385 | 385 | 589 | 629 |
| | | All | $1,090^{(-)}$ | 1,385 | $376^{(-)}$ | 464 | 733 | 786 |
| | Competitive | Joint | $7,567^{(+)}$ | 4,301 | 1,357 | 1,646 | $6,032^{(+)}$ | 2,679 |
| | | Solo | 2,763 | 2,729 | 1,090 | 1,274 | 1,871 | 1,697 |
| | | All | $4,725^{(+)}$ | 3,522 | $1,134^{(-)}$ | 1,421 | $3,117^{(+)}$ | 2,121 |
| | Aggregate | Joint | $3,844^{(+)}$ | 2,579 | $513^{(-)}$ | 1,074 | $2,572^{(+)}$ | 1,719 |
| | | Solo | $1,164^{(-)}$ | 1,575 | $520^{(-)}$ | 620 | 828 | 907 |
| | | All | 1,901 | 2,005 | $519^{(-)}$ | 757 | 1,224 | 1,187 |

[a] Significant differences in lease attributes at 95 percent level for leases involving any restricted bidder are indicated in the table using (+) or (-) superscripted signs. A (+) indicates the mean value for majors is significantly larger and a (-) that the value is significantly smaller than the mean value for leases involving non-majors only.

67

## 3.4 Conclusions

Neither aggregate measures used by economist to analyze competitive and noncompetitive market and industry structures, nor patterns of joint bidding and cooperation among firms active in the offshore Gulf of Mexico indicate or suggest a deficiency in the competitiveness of the lease sales held by MMS. Whether the measures are applied to the leases acquired at the sales, or to production by firms bidding for leases, they indicate a competitive industry bidding for leases in a competitive market.

The effects of mergers are not reflected in the trends observable in these measures over time. Although the more recent mega-mergers are only incorporated in the last two or three years of the data series analyzed, their effects will not change the quantitative measures of the competitiveness of the industry or lease market. The relative share of BP has increased dramatically as a result of the merger of BP, Amoco, Arco/Vastar, but by far the largest change in market share in the industry was the result of the growth of production by non-merger participant Shell. Other merger participants were experiencing stable or declining share of Gulf production, and their mergers did not affect overall competitiveness.

A comparison of major and non-major companies as defined by EIA criteria did not indicate any differences between the groups or their response to market structure. Similarly, an analysis of patterns of bidding by those firms on MMS' Restricted Bidders List does not indicate noncompetitive behavior. Chevron and Texaco submitted 136 joint winning bids in the four years immediately preceding their merger, but other instances of concentrated joint bidding among other firms did not lead to mergers. Further, the years in question were peak years in the leasing of the deepwater Gulf and joint bidding may have been a strategy to spread investment budgets and avoid being left out of the rush to lease. In the aggregate, however, joint bid restriction by some operators, seem to have reduced bidding effectiveness, especially, in the 1990s.

# 4. Econometric Analysis of the Market for OCS Leases

## 4.1 Model Specification

In this section we make use of two simple econometric-modeling frameworks to explore the patterns and trends in the value of OCS leases.

The first model estimates the relationship between the value of leases and postulated explanatory factors by using each of the merger and acquisition (M&A) experience categories (Groups A, B, and C, discussed previously) to estimate separate regression coefficients measuring their influence on bidding. Statistical tests then are applied to see which factors consistently influence the value of high bids on the three groups of leases.

The second model or approach uses a "major/non-major" or "restricted bidder/unrestricted bidder" delineation as a proxy for firm size, with variations of the type of bid and existence of bidding competition to form eight separate interactive variables. These are combined with merger and acquisition history or experience and other explanatory variables in a single regression equation.

Both approaches are derivative of the same basic conceptual framework, which specifies that the value of the high or winning bonus bid (HB) is a function of three sets of factors: economics, structure, and conduct. This specification has been used successfully several times in the past to analyze lease auction market performance (Dougher, 1987; Giley and Karels, 1981; Markham, 1970; Porter, 1995).

Symbolically, the general specification that has been used takes the form (Dougher, 1987; Giley and Karels, 1981; Markham, 1970):

$$HB = f(V, S, C, Z) \tag{1}$$

Where:

- $HB$ = the magnitude of the high bonus bid for a lease. This is the dependent variable in our model. It is the highest bid received and accepted by MMS for the right to develop the lease.

- $V$ represents the set of factors, which capture the expected gross value of the lease, herein referred to as "the economic factor." Some proxies that have been used in the past include:
    - Crude oil price index or current crude oil price is used as proxy for expected value of the lease in the absence of the present value of actual and future production data.
    - The number of bidders on a lease is used as a proxy for the perceived quality of the lease.

- o The number of wells drilled within 24 months has also been used to symbolize the perceived quality of leases offered.[18]

- *S* defines factors that characterize the degree of competition in the leasing program.
  - o A proxy for the intensity of competition is the number of bids or the number of bidders. It is expected that greater competition as reflected in more bids per lease is positively associated with the expected value of the high bonus bid.

- *C* is another set of factors that serve as proxies for the behavior of bidders in terms of the types of bids--joint ventures or solo, and whether the bidding was competitive, i.e. whether more than one bid for the lease was submitted.
  - o It is expected that if the incidence of joint ventures is anticompetitive, then its effect on the high bonus bid will be negative. If it is not negative, then the null hypothesis that joint venturing is anticompetitive can be rejected. The economic implication would be that, joint venturing is undertaken for information-, expertise-, or risk-sharing purposes rather than as an attempt at acquiring and applying oligopsonistic market power in the lease auctions.

- *Z* represents other variables postulated to be relevant to the value of the lease such as water depth (deep water or the shelf), the size and experience of the firm, as well as time-associated events such as the Deep Water Royalty Relief Act the U.S. Congress passed in 1995, or the collapsed of the world oil price in 1986.
  - o For deepwater leases, two factors are at work. On the one hand, other things being equal, one might expect the magnitude of the high bonus bid to decrease with water depth because of higher development costs. However, technical progress has significantly reduced finding and development costs. Along with the perception of abundant reserves, and very high production rates in deep water, this may compensate for higher development costs and lead to higher bids for deepwater reservoirs.

  - o There are reasons to expect the large firms that pioneered offshore production and have long experience in developing and producing offshore have some advantages in the bidding for OCS leases. This hypothesis will be examined by including a dummy variable to proxy the size of the firm that wins and develops the lease. If a lease is awarded to a firm or firms ranked among the top four in total production within the previous ten years, the dummy variable has a value of one; otherwise, the dummy variable has a value of zero.

  - o The historical content of lease offerings may also affect the value of the high bonus bid. For example, the collapse of the global crude oil prices in 1986 was a catastrophic economic event for those in the industry that may have negatively affected the value of high bids in subsequent years. Similarly, the passage of the Deepwater Royalty Relief Acts in by the U.S. Congress in 1999 may have had a

---

[18] Although we have tried to use previous studies as guides, for some variables, such as this one, the data either are not available or making them consistent with our data is beyond the scope of the study.

positive effect not only on net development costs but also on future expectations about the returns from developing offshore leases.

An estimable form of the functional specification in equation (1), assuming a log-linear relationship between the high bonus bid and its determinants, takes the form:

$$\ln HB_i = \alpha_{i0} + \alpha_{i1}NBD + \alpha_{i2}CPP + \alpha_{i3}DJ + \alpha_{i4}DC + \alpha_{i5}DZ + \alpha_{i6}DD + \sum_{yy}\alpha_{iy}DY + \varepsilon_{it} \tag{2}$$

Where:

*NBD* is the number of bids submitted per lease. It measures the intensity of competition for a lease. A positive relationship with the value of high bid is anticipated suggesting that the high bid value will increase as the number of bids increases, *ceteris paribus*.

*CPP* is crude petroleum price index with 1982 as the base year. It represents a measure of the perceptions or expectations prevailing in the economic environment within which the bidding process operated.

*DJ* is a dummy variable included to capture the effect of the type of high bid (whether it was a solo or a joint bid) on the value of high bid. *DJ* equals one if the lease was won through joint bid arrangement, or zero if it was won by solo bid. The inclusion of *DJ* in the model will facilitate the testing of a simple null hypothesis of whether joint bidding reflects any anticompetitive behavior in the bidding process from 1983-1999.

*DZ* is the firm size dummy variable that has the value of one if a solo bidder which ranked among the top four firms in cumulative production submitted the high bid to win the lease or if any of the bidders in a joint bid that won the lease was among the top four firms. Again the top four ranking is as defined earlier by total production in the previous ten years. Including a firm size variable enables us to reevaluate two alternative hypotheses that were postulated and tested in the early 1980s (Erickson and Spann, 1974; Giley and Karels, 1981; Markham, 1970; Mead et al., 1985). The null hypothesis is that large firms possess market power and pay less than smaller firms for leases of similar perceived quality. A significant and negative coefficient of the firm size dummy in our estimation of equation (2) will support this proposition. If, however, the coefficient is positive and significant, then the alternative hypothesis that large firms have financial or informational advantages that make it profitable to submit higher bids, all other factors accounted for cannot be rejected.

*DD* is the dummy variable for average water depth. If the average water depth is greater than 200 meters, the lease is classified as a deepwater for the purpose of this analysis.[19] *DD* is defined such that the dummy variable is equal to one if deeper than 200 meters and zero otherwise. Current technical advances tend to favor higher expectations for returns from deepwater leases as technical progress continues to drive down the cost of

---

[19] MMS's deepwater classification for ecological purposes begins at 400 meters. Other depths such as 200 meters and 800 meters are used for various regulatory purposes (MMS WebPages, January 1999).

71

exploration, completion, and production. Thus as drilling progresses into deepwater frontiers, we may experience higher bids.

*DY* is the dummy variable for the time or historical dimension. As indicated previously, this dummy can help to identify in specific terms the relative impact over time of a particular event. For example, the Deep Water Royalty Relief Act, passed in 1995 has led to, or is associated with, the subsequent, significant, increase in deepwater activity in the OCS. What happened to the value of high bids beyond the passage of this Act can be inferred from the sign of the coefficient of dummy variable capturing the time effect.

**Table 4.1** provides the definitions of the regression variables and hypothesized signs of each parameter estimate in equation 2.

## 4.2 Model Estimation and Regression Results

To estimate equation (2), a consistent database on OCS leases from published and unpublished data sources for the period 1983-1999 was constructed. The database is limited to this period to cover only the period when the area-wide-leasing policy was operational. The lease data attributes were arranged for each lease and by category of leases as previously defined.

The iterative seemingly unrelated regression (SUR) procedure in the QMS Eviews program (version 4.0) was applied to the data to estimate a log-linear specification of equation (1). SUR is employed in this study because there is a possibility of contemporaneous correlation among disturbances across different individual observations. The SUR estimator is different from OLS (ordinary least squares). Using SUR is advantageous because it is more efficient than OLS, and the gain in efficiency is positively related to the extent of correlation of the disturbances.

The log-linear specification yields parameter estimates that are interpretable as the relative change in the dependent variable with respect to an absolute change in the independent variable. **Table 4.2** presents the results of the SUR estimation of the linearized function underlying equation (1) using panel data. In general, nearly all the independent variables are statistically significant and have the expected signs.

The model is consistent with or "explains" about 50 percent of the expected variation in the relative value of high bonus bids as indicated by the $R^2$ statistics. Conversely, by implication, there are other variables not included in this model that may "explain" another 50 percent of the variation expected in the relative magnitude of high bonus bids. However, given that all the included variables are significant and the other regression statistics do not indicate any significant problem with the model's theoretical specification, the inference seems reasonable that this model captures some of the important determining factors affecting high bonus bids in the Gulf of Mexico OCS.

Table 4.1

Variable Definitions and Hypothesized Signs of the Parameters

| Determinants | Variable Name & Symbol | Parameter Symbol | Expected Sign |
|---|---|---|---|
| | Intercepts, C | $\alpha_{0i}$ | |
| Intensity of Competition | Number of Bids or Bidders, NBD | $\alpha_{1i}$ | + |
| Perceived Value of the Lease | Crude Oil Price Index, CPP | $\alpha_{2i}$ | + |
| Bidding Arrangement | Joint Ventures Dummy, DJ | $\alpha_{3i}$ | + |
| Bidding Structure | Competition Dummy, DC | $\alpha_{4i}$ | − |
| Lease Location | Deep Water Dummy, DD | $\alpha_{5i}$ | + |
| Firm Size | Top 4 Firms' Dummy, DZ | $\alpha_{6i}$ | + |
| Post Royalty Relief Act | Lease Dynamics $_{1996-1999}$ | $\alpha_{7i}$ | + |
| Post 1986 Price Effect | Lease Dynamics $_{1987-1999}$ | $\alpha_{8i}$ | − |

Table 4.2

Estimated Model of the Value of High Bonus Bids on the Gulf OCS, 1983-1999

| Determinants | i=1 Group A | i=2 Group B | i=3 Group C | Expected Sign |
|---|---|---|---|---|
| Fixed Effects | 13.6751* | 13.1264* | 12.1700* | |
| Intensity of Competition, NBD | 0.3280* | 0.3712* | 0.3451* | + |
| Economic Environment, CPP | 0.0001 | 0.0027 | 0.0189* | + |
| Bidding Arrangement, DJ | 0.2603* | 0.1826* | -0.0038 | + |
| Bidding Structure, DC | 0.3711* | 0.4223* | 0.3836* | + |
| Lease Location, DD | 0.1083* | 0.0943*** | 0.1374** | + |
| Firm Size or Experience, DZ | 0.0131 | -0.2426* | 0.3848* | − |
| Post Royalty Relief Act, DY $_{(95-99)}$ | 0.0840* | 0.0967*** | -0.1912 | + |
| Post 1986 Price Effect, DY $_{(86-99)}$ | -1.6101* | -1.3312* | -1.0549* | − |

i=1, 2, 3 for Group A, B, C leases, respectively and  *, **, *** Denotes significance at the 0.01, 0.05, 0.10 levels, respectively.

The number of bids (NBD), which measures the degree or intensity of competition, has a positive and significant effect on the value of high bids according to our regression results. This effect, in addition to the positive coefficient on DJ, provides significant evidence of competitiveness in the OCS leasing program.

As stated earlier the expected gross value of lease may be captured by the expected price of crude petroleum (as measured in crude oil price index). The sign of the estimated coefficients of the proxy for economic effect in the regression results although positive, is statistically insignificant for categories A and B.

Any inference that economic conditions or expectations are not related to the bidding for leases should be tempered by the relationship measured by the variable $DY$. The dummy variable for time, $DY$, shows all yearly dummies except those defined for the period from 1983 to 1985 and indicates a different pattern of effect on the value of high bonus bids than the periods after 1986 (the base year). Specifically, the results imply that bonus bids after 1986 tends to be lower than in the pre-1986 magnitude, taking all other influences captured in the regression equation into consideration. This is certainly consistent with the conventional wisdom among oil and gas industry participants and analysts who believe strongly that firms became much more cautious about long-term investment decisions after the collapse of the oil market in 1986.

The sign on the dummy variable $DJ$ capturing the type of the high bid (whether joint or solo) is positive and significant. Thus, the null hypothesis that joint bidding depresses high bids in lease sales is rejected. The results suggest that the incidence of joint bidding during the period of our analysis (1983-1999) shows no anti-competitive behavior or pattern during OCS lease sales.

The lease location or water depth variable, $DD$, in our regression indicates whether the fact that the lease is 200 meters or more below the surface affects the value of the high bid. It might be expected that the sign on this variable would be positive--deepwater leases increase development costs and lead to lower bids, *ceteris paribus*. On the other hand, all other things still being equal, if success rates and the size of discoveries are higher in deepwater than on the shelf, firms may bid higher for deepwater leases. The result here is consistent with the latter case, that is, the greater the water depth, the higher the bonus bids.

The coefficients for the firm-size variable $DZ$ are mixed among the three groups. Although the $DZ$ variable, which measures the relationship between large firms and high bids is statistically significant for Groups B and C, it is negative for Group B and positive for Group C. Further it is not significant for Group A. This indicates that larger firms with merger and acquisition histories and experience tend to make lower winning bids in comparison to other firms with similar histories.

In general, the results in **Table 4.2** confirm the following expectations:

- Greater competition is associated with higher mean values of high bonus bids. As competition increases, the relative change in the mean value of high bonus bids increases.

- The economic environment measured in terms of the rising crude petroleum prices does not lead to a significantly higher mean value of high bids for most leases, as most probably would have expected. However, another measure of perceptions of the economic environment, the carry-over effects of the collapse of crude oil prices in 1986 which brought about major strategic and structural changes in the global E&P industry, does consistently indicate a significant reduction in the mean value of high bonus bids for leases in comparison to the pre-1986 mean value of high bids. A more descriptively accurate way to view this relationship may be that the run-up in world oil prices in the beginning of the 1980s has an aberration based on unrealistic expectations. After the price collapse, expectations resumed more realistic and modest levels.

- The mean value of high bonus bids for leases with at least two bids (competitive) is greater than the mean value of single-bid leases (noncompetitive).

- The mean value of high bonus bids for deepwater leases is significantly higher than shallow water leases.

- Joint venturing is associated significantly with higher winning bonus bids than is the case for bids by solo ventures.

## 4.3 Effects of Mergers and Acquisitions on the Value of OCS Leases

To decipher the potential effects of merger and acquisitions on the mean value of high bonus bids through its determinants--intensity of competition, extent of competition, type of bid, lease location/water depth, economics, and structural changes in the E&P industry--a Wald coefficient restriction test was applied to the regression results in **Table 4.2.**

A Wald test ascertains if the coefficients measuring the relationship between the explanatory variables and the average high bid for the three groups are significantly different from one another. The objective of employing the test here is to ascertain which influences on high bids seem to be affected by M&A experience and which do not.

Subsequently, equation (2) was estimated again, using the same data set but, with restrictions imposed on the parameters measuring the relationship of the change in high bid value to changes the variables that the Wald test indicated were not significantly different from each other for the three groups specifically, intensity of competition, extent of competition, and lease location/water depth. Symbolically, the new regression equation specified that:

$\alpha_{1i} = \alpha_1$ for $i = 1, 2, 3$, $\alpha_{4i} = \alpha_4$ for $i = 1, 2, 3$, and $\alpha_{5i} = \alpha_5$ for $i = 1, 2, 3$.

The restricted regression model results are presented in **Table 4.3**. It should be noted that the signs of the estimated model parameters did not change after imposing the Wald restrictions. Neither were there any changes with respect to the results of our tests of significance of the estimates nor the adjusted $R^2$.

The following observations or statistical inferences are plausible concerning the overall effects of mergers and acquisitions on the market for OCS oil and gas leases using the results reported in **Table 4.3**:

Table 4.3

Estimated Model of the Value of High Bonus Bids with Coefficient Restrictions

| Determinants | i=1 Group A | i=2 Group B | i=3 Group C | Expected Sign |
|---|---|---|---|---|
| Fixed Effects | 13.6714* | 13.1628* | 12.1758* | |
| Intensity of Competition, *NBD* | 0.3323* | 0.3323* | 0.3323* | + |
| Economic Environment, *CPP* | 0.0000 | 0.0027 | 0.0192* | + |
| Bidding Type, *DJ* | 0.2589* | 0.1981* | 0.0028 | + |
| Bidding Competition, *DC* | 0.3771* | 0.3771* | 0.3771* | + |
| Lease Location, *DD* | 0.1093* | 0.1093* | 0.1093* | + |
| Firm Size, *DZ* | 0.0138 | -0.2409* | 0.3801* | − |
| Post Royalty Relief Act, *DY* $_{(95-99)}$ | 0.0831* | 0.0990 | -0.1810 | + |
| Post 1986 Price Effect, *DY* $_{(86-99)}$ | -1.6115* | -1.3233* | -1.0412* | − |

- Mergers and acquisitions, as indicated by differences between the coefficients for Group B and Groups A and C, do not significantly alter the overall expectation that intensity of competition for OCS leases leads to a higher mean value of winning bonus bids, *ceteris paribus*. In other words, the relative change in the mean value of high bonus bids per unit change in the number of bids per lease is not significantly affected when firms that have been involved in M&A participated in the high bonus bids. The intensity of competition for a lease has a positive, strong, and significant effect on the magnitude of the winning bid, but it is not affected by M&A experience, i.e., it affects all three groups to the same degree.

- The percent increase in the mean value of high bonus bids for leases that received at least two bids (competitive leases) over noncompetitive leases is not significantly affected by M&A experience. As with the intensity of competition variable, the relationship between high bids and whether or not there are competing bidders is strong and significant but the same for all three groups.

- The increase in the relative mean value of the high bonus bid for deep water leases over the leases in the shelf is about 11 percent and this is not significantly affected by M&A bidders' participation in the high bonus bid. Again, it affects all three groups to the same degree.

- The involvement of bidders ranking as the top four firms in cumulative production significantly leads to a lower relative value of high bids in the Group B leases. Whereas the expected mean value of high bonus bids for Group A and C leases involving bidders ranked among the top four is not significantly different from other bidders, i.e., non-top-four bidders.

- On average, the relative value of high bonus bids has dropped significantly since the collapse of world crude oil prices and the decline is significantly different among the three groups. The effect is strong in all three groups but is less so for leases in which participating firms had been involved in or would become involved in M&A activities.

- The parameters designated as fixed effects (intercepts) are significantly different in magnitude, thus suggesting that the relative change in the mean value of high bonus bids for OCS leases, *ceteris paribus*, was on average relatively smaller for leases in which participating bidders include a firm or firms involved in M&A plan over the entire period 1983-1999, when other factors have been accounted for. This result could be interpreted as suggesting these firms were able to exercise some degree of oligopsony power as a consequence of M&A activities, or as suggesting that this group of firms possessed better information or had more experience, which enabled them to bid more efficiently. Since the competitive measures indicate no significant difference among the three categories, the second interpretation is more consistent with our data.

## 4.4 Firms of Different Sizes and the Value of OCS Oil and Gas Leases

*Effects of Majors and Non-majors*: The purpose of this section is to evaluate the same relationships discussed in the previous section, but to use the distinction between "major" and "non-major" or the distinction between "restricted bidders" and "unrestricted bidders" rather than M&A experience as a tool to do so. Although a different formulation and estimation of equation (1) is adopted, we are concerned with the same measures of the behavior and performance of firms in OCS oil and gas lease auction markets as we were previously. For example, did major oil operators on the OCS traditionally pay more for competitive joint venture leases than for competitive solo venture leases? Or do majors pay less than non-majors for competitive joint venture leases?

The formulation or approach used in this section is similar to the one used in Mead et al. (1985) in which different possible categories of leases were selected based on the size of bidders involved in the high bonus bids, the lease type and bidding arrangement. Thus, using Mead's approach, a set of interactive dummy variables was employed to define eight distinct combinations of: 1) type of bid (joint or solo), 2) extent or existence of competition in bidding, and 3) firm size, but using the major/non-major classification as a proxy.

Using this format, the eight possible lease categories are:

- *MJC*: High bonus bids which involved major oil and gas operators, bidding jointly for competitive leases.

- *MJN*: High bonus bids which involved major oil and gas operators, bidding jointly for noncompetitive leases.

- *MSC*: High bonus bids which involved major oil and gas operators, bidding solo for competitive leases.

- *MSN*: High bonus bids which involved major oil and gas operators, bidding solo for noncompetitive leases.

- *NMJC*: High bonus bids involving non-major oil and gas operators only, bidding jointly for competitive leases.

- *NMJN*: High bonus bids involving non-major oil and gas operators, bidding jointly for noncompetitive leases.

- *NMSC*: High bonus bids involving non-major oil and gas operators, bidding solo for competitive leases.

- *NMSN*: High bonus bids involving non-major oil and gas operators, bidding solo for noncompetitive leases.

The estimated results of Equation 2 using covariance-pooling techniques (CAT) and different base cases are reported in **Tables 4.4** and **4.5**. The estimated equation includes new sets of dummy variables used as proxies for the eight categories of leases representing the different set of lease combinations, which were listed above. The CAT estimation techniques allow for cross-sectional differences or inter-temporal differences with restrictive assumptions that some of the slope coefficients are equal and stochastic, and that at least one of the intercepts is different and stochastic.

In general, the base case results presented in **Table 4.4** are consistent with and strengthen the results from the SUR formulation based summarized in **Tables 4.2** and **4.3**. Specifically, the CAT results using non-major, noncompetitive solo venture bids as the base case also show:

- As competition increases, the relative change in (the natural logarithm of) the mean value of high bonus bids also increases.

- The diminished expectations that followed the collapse of crude oil prices in 1986, depresses the mean value of high bonus bids for leases in a manner that is very consistent with the SUR results.

- The mean value of high bonus bids for deep-water leases is significantly higher than for shallow water leases, *ceteris paribus*.

- A negative or inverse relationship between the value of the high bids and bidders who have been involved in mergers and acquisitions.

- A positive effect from the Deepwater Royalty Relief Acts of 1995.

The only difference between the SUR results reported in Section 4 and the CAT results, is a small positive effect of rising crude petroleum prices on the mean value high bonus bids of leases as would have been expected, but only at a 90 percent confidence level.

Table 4.4

Estimated CAT Model of the Relative Change in the
Value of High Bonus Bids with NMSN as the Base Case[a]

| Determinants | Parameter Estimate | Std. Error | A priori Sign |
|---|---|---|---|
| Intercept | 13.4846* | 0.0732 | |
| Intensity of Competition, NBD | 0.3326* | 0.0111 | + |
| Economic Environment, CPP | 0.0015*** | 0.0008 | + |
| Interactive D1 Variable, MJC | 0.7117* | 0.0403 | |
| Interactive D2 Variable, MJN | 0.3430* | 0.0278 | |
| Interactive D3 Variable, MSC | 0.5169* | 0.0344 | |
| Interactive D4 Variable, MSN | 0.1432* | 0.0227 | |
| Interactive D5 Variable, NMJC | 0.6887* | 0.0426 | |
| Interactive D6 Variable, NMJN | 0.3385* | 0.0322 | |
| Interactive D7 Variable, NMSC | 0.3898* | 0.0388 | |
| Deepwater Lease Dummy, DDP | 0.0820* | 0.0168 | + |
| Merger & Acquisition Dummy, DMA | -0.2177* | 0.0263 | |
| Post Royalty Relief Act, $DY_{(95-99)}$ | 0.1000* | 0.0176 | + |
| Post 1986 Price Collapse, $DY_{(86-99)}$ | -1.5807* | 0.0323 | − |

*, **, *** Denotes significance at the 0.01, 0.05, 0.10 levels, respectively.
[a]The base case represents leases won through noncompetitive solo venture bids by firms classified as non-major oil and gas operators only (NMSN).

Table 4.5

Estimated Model of the Relative Change in the
Value of High Bonus Bids with Varying Base Case[1]

| | MJC | MJN | MSC | MSN | NMJC | NMJN | NMSC | NMSN |
|---|---|---|---|---|---|---|---|---|
| MJC | | -0.369* | -0.195* | -0.568* | -0.023 | -0.373* | -0.322* | -0.712* |
| MJN | 0.369* | | 0.174* | -0.200* | 0.345* | -0.005 | 0.047 | -0.343* |
| MSC | 0.195* | -0.174* | | -0.374* | 0.172* | -0.178* | -0.127* | -0.517* |
| MSN | 0.568* | 0.200* | 0.374* | | 0.545* | 0.195* | 0.247* | -0.143* |
| NMJC | 0.023 | -0.346* | -0.172* | -0.545* | | -0.350* | -0.299* | -0.689* |
| NMJN | 0.373* | 0.005 | 0.178* | -0.195* | 0.350* | | 0.051 | -0.338* |
| NMSC | 0.322* | -0.047 | 0.127* | -0.247* | 0.299* | -0.051 | | -0.390* |
| NMSN | 0.712* | 0.343* | 0.517* | 0.143* | 0.689* | 0.338* | 0.390* | |

*, **, *** Denotes significance at the 0.01, 0.05, 0.10 levels, respectively.
[1]The varying base case represents each possible lease combinations on the basis of the classification of the firms involved in the winning bids (M or NM), the bidding type (J or S) or bidding structure (C or N).

Given our objectives in this report, the most relevant results are:

- The inverse relationship between *DMA (*M&A history and experience), and the average level of high bids, which supports the previous findings that firms with a history of M&A, on average, submit lower winning bids (other factors taken into account) than firms that have not.

- Comparisons of the coefficients and the comparisons of the differences among coefficients of the interactive dummy variables, D1 through D7.

The comparisons of the coefficients is facilitated by **Table 4.5** which presents the relative differences in the expected lease value in a relative term between lease categories with varying base case specification. The numbers reported under the columns in **Table 4.5** are the parameter estimates of the effect of the interactive dummy represented in the column on the relative change in the mean value of the high bonus with respect to the base case lease category represented by each row in the table. The relative confidence levels for ascertaining the statistical significance of the differences among the variables are also shown in the table.

Comparisons of interest include:

- All of the interactive dummy variables for majors have larger coefficients than the corresponding combination including only non-majors, i.e., D1 (*MJC)*>D5 (*NMJC), D2* > D6, D3>D7. However the differences are significant (as indicated in **Table 4.5**) only for solo bids, both those that are competitive and those that are not. This suggests that if firm size, as measured by the major/non-major classification, has any effect on bidding it is a positive effect.

- The fact that there is no significant difference between joint bids involving majors and joint bids not involving majors, i.e., *MJC and NMJC, or MJN and NMJN,* supports skepticism about the rationale for the Restricted Bidders List approach for discouraging anti-competitive behavior through restrictions on joint bidding discussed in the second chapter of the report.

- Within both the major and the non-major classifications, competitive bids are consistently and significantly higher than noncompetitive bids, reinforcing the results of previous sections.

***Effects of Joint Bid Restrictions:*** In this section, we will evaluate the effect of joint bid restriction on the market for OCS oil and gas leases using equation (2). A new set of databases is constructed for this purpose using MMS' Restricted Bidders List from 1983-1999, lease structure (ex post) and bidding arrangement or type. As previously stated, we are again concerned with the same measures of the behavior and performance of firms in OCS oil and gas lease auction markets. For example, was the value of leases involving restricted joint bidders on the OCS traditionally more than leases involving nonrestricted bidders? Or do restricted bidders pay less than non restricted for joint venture leases irrespective of the ex post lease structure?

A set of interactive dummy variables was again employed to define eight distinct combinations of: 1) type of bid (joint or solo), 2) extent or existence of competition in bidding, and 3) firm size, but using the restricted/nonrestricted classification as a proxy.

Using this format, the eight possible lease categories are:

- *RJC*: High bonus bids which involved restricted bidders, bidding jointly for competitive leases (leases which received at least two bids).

- *RJN*: High bonus bids which involved restricted bidders, bidding jointly for noncompetitive leases (leases which received only one bid).

- *RSC*: High bonus bids which involved restricted bidders, bidding solo for leases receiving at least two bids (competitive leases).

- *RSN*: High bonus bids which involved restricted bidders, bidding solo for leases receiving at least two bids (noncompetitive leases).

- *UJC*: High bonus bids involving unrestricted bidders, bidding jointly for competitive leases (leases which received at least two bids).

- *UJN*: High bonus bids involving unrestricted bidders, bidding jointly for noncompetitive leases (leases which received only one bid).

- *USC*: High bonus bids involving unrestricted bidders, bidding solo for leases receiving at least two bids (competitive leases).

- *USN*: High bonus bids involving non-major oil and gas operators, bidding solo for leases receiving at least two bids (noncompetitive leases).

In general, the base case results presented in **Table 4.6** using covariance-pooling techniques (CAT) restricted/unrestricted bidder classification of leases are similar to the results summarized in **Table 4.4**. The only noticeable exception is the negative and statistically significant index of economic environment, which is contrary to our a priori positive expectations. Although this index has an expected positive sign in the two previous results, it was only marginally significant at the 10 percent level.

The CAT results using unrestricted, noncompetitive solo venture bids as the base case also show:

- As competition increases, the relative change in (the natural logarithm of) the mean value of high bonus bids also increases.

- The diminished expectations that followed the collapse of crude oil prices in 1986, depresses the mean value of high bonus bids for leases in a manner that is consistent with earlier results.

81

Table 4.6

Estimated CAT Model of the Relative Change in the
Value of High Bonus Bids with *USN* as the Base Case[a]

| Determinants | Parameter Estimate | Std. Error | A priori Sign |
|---|---|---|---|
| Intercept | 13.9397* | 0.0844 | |
| Intensity of Competition, *NBD* | 0.3324* | 0.0114 | + |
| Economic Environment, *CPP* | -0.0028* | 0.0009 | + |
| Interactive D1 Variable, *RJC* | 0.6706* | 0.0437 | |
| Interactive D2 Variable, *RJN* | 0.1472* | 0.0353 | |
| Interactive D3 Variable, *RSC* | 0.4944* | 0.0358 | |
| Interactive D4 Variable, *RSN* | 0.0764* | 0.0225 | |
| Interactive D5 Variable, *UJC* | 0.6325* | 0.0374 | |
| Interactive D6 Variable, *UJN* | 0.3338* | 0.0235 | |
| Interactive D7 Variable, *USC* | 0.3617* | 0.0337 | |
| Deepwater Dummy, *DDP* | 0.1000* | 0.0171 | + |
| Merger & Acquisition Dummy, *DMA* | -0.1574* | 0.0235 | |
| Post Royalty Relief Act, *DY* (95-99) | 0.0445* | 0.0179 | + |
| Post 1986 Price Collapse, *DY* (86-99) | -1.704* | 0.0378 | − |

*, **, *** Denotes significance at the 0.01, 0.05, 0.10 levels, respectively.
[a]The base case represents leases won through noncompetitive solo venture bids by firms classified as unrestricted bidders only *(USN)*.

- The mean value of high bonus bids for deep-water leases is significantly higher than for shallow water leases, *ceteris paribus*.

- A negative or inverse relationship between the value of the high bids and bidders who have been involved in mergers and acquisitions.

- A positive effect from the Deepwater Royalty Relief Acts of 1995.

Given our objectives of this report, the econometric analysis in this section using restricted and unrestricted classification still confirms a statistically significant inverse relationship between *DMA* (M&A history and experience), and the average level of high bids. The results support the previous findings that firms with history of M&A, on average, submit lower winning bids (other factors taken into account) than firms that have not.

**Table 4.7** presents the relative differences in the expected lease value in a relative term between lease categories with varying base case specification. As previously stated, the numbers reported under the columns in **Table 4.7** are measures of the effect of the interactive dummy represented in the column with respect to the base case lease category represented by each row in the table. The relative confidence levels for ascertaining the statistical significance of the differences among the variables are also shown in the table.

Table 4.7

Estimated Model of the Relative Change in the
Value of High Bonus Bids with Varying Base Case[1]

|  | RJC | RJN | RSC | RSN | UJC | UJN | USC | USN |
|---|---|---|---|---|---|---|---|---|
| RJC |  | -0.523* | -0.159* | -0.594* | -0.038 | -0.337* | -0.331* | -0.671* |
| RJN | 0.523* |  | 0.347* | -0.071*** | 0.485* | 0.187* | 0.215* | -0.147* |
| RSC | 0.159* | -0.347* |  | -0.418* | 0.138* | -0.161* | -0.172* | -0.494* |
| RSN | 0.594* | 0.071*** | 0.418* |  | 0.556* | 0.257* | 0.285* | -0.076* |
| UJC | 0.038 | -0.485* | -0.138* | -0.556* |  | -0.299* | -0.269* | -0.633* |
| UJN | 0.337* | -0.187* | 0.161* | -0.257* | 0.299* |  | 0.032 | -0.334* |
| USC | 0.331* | -0.215* | 0.172* | -0.285* | 0.269* | -0.032 |  | -0.362* |
| USN | 0.671* | 0.147* | 0.494* | 0.076* | 0.633* | 0.334* | 0.362* |  |

*, **, *** Denotes significance at the 0.01, 0.05, 0.10 levels, respectively.
[1]The varying base case (row) represents each possible lease combinations on the basis of the classification of the firms involved in the winning bids (U or R), the bidding type (J or S) or bidding structure (C or N).

It can be inferred from the table that:

All of the interactive dummy variables for majors have larger coefficients than the corresponding combination including only non-majors, i.e., D1 (*MJC*)>D5 (*NMJC*), D2 > D6, D3>D7. However the differences are significant (as indicated in **Table 4.5**) only for solo bids, both those that are competitive and those that are not. This suggests that if firm size, as measured by the major/non-major classification, has any effect on bidding it is a positive effect.

- There is no significant difference between competitive joint bids involving restricted bidders and joint bids not involving restricted bidders, i.e., *RJC* and *UJC*. However, when joint bidding is for leases classified *ex post* as noncompetitive, the bids are significantly less if restricted bidders are involved, i.e. *RJN* < *UJN*.

- Within both the restricted and the unrestricted firm classifications, competitive bids are consistently and significantly higher than noncompetitive bids.

- Within both the restricted and the unrestricted firm classifications, joint venture bids for under comparative ex post bidding structure (competitive or non competitive) are consistently and significantly higher than solo venture bids, reinforcing the results of previous sections (*RJC>RSC, RJN > RSN, UJC>USC,* and *UJN>USN*).

These results suggest some skepticism about the rationale for the Restricted Bidders List approach for discouraging anti-competitive behavior through restrictions on joint bidding discussed in the second chapter of the report.

# 5. Conclusions and Implications

The core of our study is an analysis of leasing of offshore oil and gas property under the jurisdiction of the Minerals Management Service since the adoption of area-wide leasing in 1983. Our study is a broad application of statistical measurements and techniques to a large number of transactions involving a complex and evolving set of firms either acting alone or jointly with other firms, over a time period of major changes in the industry and its economic, political and technological context. It is an analytical overview, not a dispositive analysis.

None of the measures of industrial concentration indicate that the characteristics of the offshore lease auction/market exceed criteria used to characterize concentrated or potentially uncompetitive industries. Econometric analyses following different approaches and formulations do not reveal a negative association between the size of firms and average winning bids. The association is either statistically insignificant or positive, suggesting larger firms submit higher average bids when other contextual variables are incorporated into the analysis.

However the variables measuring whether or not firms have participated in mergers or acquisitions before the time of the lease sale, consistently show a modest negative relationship between average high bids and merger and acquisition experience or history. Such an association could be interpreted as evidence that firms who have participated in mergers or acquisitions have, in some way, either acquired a degree of oligopsonistic market power or tend to be better informed or more experienced and, thus, more efficient bidders. We find the latter a more plausible conjecture.

Although we have identified and characterized some patterns of bidding on a less aggregated basis, an adequate analysis of this subject exceeds the scope of, and resources available for, the project. However, the weight of the evidence in our view is that the lease market is competitive and that there are no apparent barriers to its efficient operation.

A related implication of our analysis is that Restricted Bidders List that MMS is required to prepare does not appear to serve a useful public policy purpose. The criteria used to compile the list are arbitrary and the list has not been used in other legal or regulatory determinations by MMS or the Department of Justice. Joint bidding is consistently associated with higher average winning bids and seems to be consistent with, and perhaps enhanced by competition in the lease market.

# 6. References

Baud, R.D., et al. 2002. Deepwater Gulf of Mexico 2002: America's Expanding Frontier, OCS Report MMS 2002-021. New Orleans: Minerals Management Service.

Brennan, M.J. and T.M. Carroll. 1987. *Preface to Quantitative Economics and Econometrics*. Cincinnati: South-Western Publishing Co.

Dougher, R. 1987. Market Shares and Individual Company Data for the U.S. Energy Markets 1950-1986, Discussion Paper #014R. Washington, DC: American Petroleum Institute.

Erickson, E.W. and R.M. Spann. 1974. An Analysis of the Competitive Effects of Joint Ventures in the Bidding for Tracts in OCS Offshore Lease Sales. In: *Hearings before the Special Subcommittee on Integrated Oil Operations of the Senate Committee on Committee on Interior and Insular Affairs, Market Performance and Competition in the Oil Industry*. Washington, DC: U.S. Government Printing Office.

Gilley, O. and G. Karels. 1981. The Competitive Effects in Bonus Bidding, New Evidence. *Bell Journal of Economics* 12(2):637-648.

Iledare, O.O., A.G. Pulsipher, and R.H. Bauman. 1995. Effects of an Increasing Role for Independents on Petroleum Development. *The Energy Journal* 16(2):59-76.

Markham, J.W. 1970. The Competitive Effects of Joint Bidding by Oil Companies for Offshore Leases. In: Markham, J.W. and G.F. Papanek, eds. *Industrial Organization and Economic Development: In Honor of E.S. Mason*. Boston, MA: Houghton Mifflin.

McDonald, S.L. 1979. *The Leasing of Federal Lands for Fossil Fuels Production*. Baltimore: Johns Hopkins University Press.

Mead, W.J., A. Moseidjord, D. Mauraoka, and P.E. Sorensen. 1985. *Offshore Lands: Oil and Gas leasing and Conservation on the Outer Continental Shelf*. Pacific Institute for Public Policy Research.

Mead, W.J. and P.E. Sorensen. 1980. Competition and Performance in OCS Oil and Gas Lease and Lease Development, 1954-1969. Final Report to the U.S. Geological Survey, Reston, VA. Contract #14-08-0001-16552.

Millsaps, S.W. and M. Ott. 1981. Information and Bidding Behavior by Major Oil Companies for Outer Continental Shelf Leases: Is the Joint Bidding Ban Justified? *The Energy Journal* 2(1):71-190.

Moody, C.E. and W.J. Kruvant. 1990. OCS Leasing Policy and Lease Prices. *Land Economics* 66(1).

Moody, C.E. and W.J. Kruvant. 1988. Joint Bidding, Entry, and the Price of OCS Leases. *Rand Journal of Economics* 19:276-284.

Petroleum Industry Research Foundation. 2002. *Refining Concentration and Industry Dynamics.* New York: Petroleum Industry Research Foundation, Inc. (PIRINC).

Porter, R.H. 1995. The Role of Information in U.S. Offshore Oil and Gas Lease Auctions. *Econometricia* 63(1):1-27.

Rockwood, A. 1983. The Impact of Joint Ventures on the Market for OCS Oil and Gas Leases. *Journal of Industrial Economics* 31(4):453-468.

Saidi, R. and J.R. Marsden. 1992. Number of Bids, Number of Bidders and Bidding Behavior in Outer Continental Shelf Oil Lease Auctions. *European Journal of Operations Research.* Pp. 335-343.

Sullivan, B. and P. Kobrin. 1980. The Joint Bidding Ban: Pro- and Anti-Competitive Theories of Joint Bidding in OCS Lease Sales. *Journal of Economics and Business* 33(1):1-19.

Teisberg, T.J. 1980. Federal Management of Energy and Mineral Resources on the Public Land. *Bell Journal of Economics* 11:448-465.

U.S. Department of Energy, Energy Information Administration. 2002. *Performance Profiles of Major Energy Producers 2000.* DOE/EIA-0206 (00). Washington, DC: U.S. Government Printing Office.

## The Department of the Interior Mission

As the Nation's principal conservation agency, the Department of the Interior has responsibility for most of our nationally owned public lands and natural resources. This includes fostering sound use of our land and water resources; protecting our fish, wildlife, and biological diversity; preserving the environmental and cultural values of our national parks and historical places; and providing for the enjoyment of life through outdoor recreation. The Department assesses our energy and mineral resources and works to ensure that their development is in the best interests of all our people by encouraging stewardship and citizen participation in their care. The Department also has a major responsibility for American Indian reservation communities and for people who live in island territories under U.S. administration.

## The Minerals Management Service Mission

As a bureau of the Department of the Interior, the Minerals Management Service's (MMS) primary responsibilities are to manage the mineral resources located on the Nation's Outer Continental Shelf (OCS), collect revenue from the Federal OCS and onshore Federal and Indian lands, and distribute those revenues.

Moreover, in working to meet its responsibilities, the **Offshore Minerals Management Program** administers the OCS competitive leasing program and oversees the safe and environmentally sound exploration and production of our Nation's offshore natural gas, oil and other mineral resources. The MMS **Minerals Revenue Management** meets its responsibilities by ensuring the efficient, timely and accurate collection and disbursement of revenue from mineral leasing and production due to Indian tribes and allottees, States and the U.S. Treasury.

The MMS strives to fulfill its responsibilities through the general guiding principles of: (1) being responsive to the public's concerns and interests by maintaining a dialogue with all potentially affected parties and (2) carrying out its programs with an emphasis on working to enhance the quality of life for all Americans by lending MMS assistance and expertise to economic development and environmental protection.

www.ingramcontent.com/pod-product-compliance
Lightning Source LLC
Chambersburg PA
CBHW052004280526
45793CB00005B/846